UNSPIRITUALITY
PERMISSION TO BE HUMAN

Copyright © 2013 by Christopher Loren
Createspace Independent Publishing Platform
2nd edition August 6, 2013

All rights reserved
Printed in the United States of America
Second Edition

ISBN-13: 978-1484005125
ISBN-10: 1484005120

For more information about permission to reproduce selections from this book, send email to Christopher Loren on contact page at the Website. unSpirituality.com

ChristopherZzennLoren.com

Special Thanks

To those friends and acquaintances who contributed to making this book possible by challenging my ideas and contributing their talents.

And to those spiritual seekers who continue to embrace the curiosity and wonderment of a child.

You are truly The Imaginarians.

Dedication

This book is dedicated to my species and all who have come before. To the innumerable who suffered under the tyranny of dualism, your time has come.

And to the children of hereditary religious or spiritual ideology, *never let go of your gut feeling*. Your natural intelligence is yours to keep. Trust your experience and honor your innate curiosity—it is there for a reason!

I wrote this for you.

Note to the Reader

The content in this book is addressing the ideology of religious and spiritual belief. The challenge set forth is to redefine metaphysical realities in light of the natural world. In this writing, I attempt to delineate the individual *apart from* the content of the imagination in its religious-spiritual form; that being, a human primate instead of a soul existing inside a body. By no means is this writing meant to assign blame or judgment against the individual. Rather, I focus the charge on the spiritual ego to bring it into the light. Regarding science, I make references throughout the book on scientific studies, but in no way do I consider science to be the end all of human understanding. It is simply a tool for understanding our universe, one that has proven itself profoundly useful to our species. There are as many theories as there are scientists and yet some theories have proven the test of time—evolution is one of them. *I also believe we have yet to truly understand our subjective connection to nature.* I spent most of my life walking the spiritual path and I come to this writing, humbly, as one who has been there. If you are a believer in spiritual realms, I encourage you to read on, even if the content challenges your beliefs. It is my hope, that by the end of this book, everything that you have experienced under the spiritual banner will be enhanced by redefining it through the natural world.

I invite you to a new perspective.

Contents

Forward by Robert Mark	11
Introduction	13
Insert - I Am Primate	17

UNSPIRITUALITY

1.	Bamboozled	21
2.	Defining Spirituality	27
3.	The Never-Ending Story	35
4.	The Invisible Self	47

THE SUBJECTIVE

5.	Imagination	59
6.	Emotion	67
7.	Identification	73
8.	Childhood Trauma	81

Insert - Planet of Lost Primates   89

I AM HUMAN

9.	The Human Animal	93
10.	Unfathomable Evolution	99
11.	Natural Intelligence	105

Insert - A Spiritual Conspiracy   111

THE GREAT DELUSION

12.	The New Prejudice	115
13.	Denying the Natural	123
14.	Plagiarizing Nature	135
15.	Divine Narcissism	141
16.	Obsessed with the Invisible	147

Insert - Revelations of a Zombie   153

SOFT LANDING

    17. Natural Love   159
    18. Understanding the Subjective   169
    19. Living in Real Time   177
    20. The Focusing Method   185

Conclusion   191
Insert – Healing Our World   195

Forward

Christopher Loren's "unSpirituality: Permission to be Human" breaks new ground in the growing sense that we've been sold down the river of false hope and illusion for many centuries. My book, "Clearing the Path: Opening the Spiritual Frontier," is a soft nudge to all those interested in shifting away from the "God owns you, so do what we tell you" mythology, or the "do not think for yourself" instructions to stay dumb, live in denial, and hide what you know.

Christopher's treatise is a battering ram at the doors of illusion, repression, subjugation and subservience to the religious conspirators, religious mega-corporations and religious power-seekers of our time. He has lived a life that led him down the pathways of belief and myth. A journey that never quite matched up with his native common sense, until, having accumulated a wealth of experience, was able to put it all together and release himself from the shackles of metaphysical ignorance.

Now, in his first book, Christopher takes his journey to the reader. His language powerfully opens the reader's eyes and heart to their own suspicions, and gut feelings, about the insidious and destructive games that have been played upon the board of mankind throughout our history and within all cultures. The very things that each religion thinks are unique about their "story" can be found in virtually all religious themes around the world. This might lead some to believe that this is an indication of the universal truth of the story. What it really points to, however, is the truth of the psyche of the time that led some to need a universal over-lord belief. This need for belief was used by the religious authorities to convince others to follow their own megalomaniacal quest for power and control. Over time the distortions of those early beliefs have only made things worse.

As I indicated in my book, isn't it strange to think that the singular God entity of a religion that is practiced all over the world is capable of understanding prayers coming to him (or her) in all these different languages, while honing in with precision via some divine GPS, so that your specific prayer can be answered and not get confused with another person's petitions? The conspirators would simply say, "well, that's the magnificence of the all-knowing, all-seeing one." Christopher would say, "give us a break, that's a bunch of hooey" and go on to demonstrate what that hooey has done to mankind.

I strongly encourage you to read this book, to make notes on stick-ums, and attach them to the pages for future forehead smacking reminders of your ah-ha moments.

—Robert Mark Ph. D.
Author of Clearing the Path: Opening the Spiritual Frontier.

INTRODUCTION

*"The image of God is the final obstruction.
God is the ultimate barrier."*

—Joseph Campbell

In 1993, at the age of 29, I had a sense that one day I would write a book. Now, this writing has arrived at a time when spiritual thought is being challenged through the voice of reason. It was always my intent to write something that would alter the way humans perceive reality in lieu of our past assumptions. This is a big task and I am humbled to have the opportunity to share my voice regarding a topic that has held a majority seat in the consciousness of mankind.

UnSpirituality is a word that falls under the same banner as naturalism. It points toward a human form of spirituality, one that is biological. I chose this word because it reverses the meaning assigned to spirituality over the centuries—dualism. Dualism is the belief that there is a "soul in a body with a story" that extends beyond the natural world.

UnSpirituality represents the antithesis to metaphysical ideology. This word, by itself, was not enough, it was missing something vital to the completion of an idea. The idea was to redirect the light that spirituality placed on the invisible and turn it back toward the natural—the mortal primate and its evolutionary origins. Thus, the subtitle "Permission to Be Human" in big bold letters was added to complete the message.

When 'Permission to Be Human' was added to the title of the website (unSpirituality.com), I felt as if a combination lock had clicked, perfectly completing a feeling I have come to recognize as *true*. At the time, I had not yet conceived of the book you are holding in your hands. I had just begun writing the story of my spiritual journey to create a backdrop from which to write about the insights gained from my life experience; a story of childhood trauma and the effects religion and spirituality have on the recovering adult. It is the saga of one person's fight for the right to think, feel, and be as they naturally are free from the dictates of cultural programming and metaphysical thought, taking the reader beyond the whisper of the inner child to the defiant shout of a free mind.

However, I decided to write the second book first because I felt the message was more pressing than the story, like an urgency in my skin, a primal scream waiting to be released from the spiritual prison it had been sentenced. I observed the subtle discontent in the eyes of my friends who lived in a town well known for its spiritual reputation—Sedona, Arizona—global hot spot for all things unseen.

So, I decided to write this book for my friends, family and anyone else who was willing to look at their spiritual lives from a different perspective; one that was natural and physical, rather than supernatural and invisible. Because of my forty-year subjective imprisonment there are moments in this writing where readers will hear the "rage against the machine" tone behind my prose. I make no apology for this because I believe there are many who have not yet discovered their own voice and might experience their reflection in my words. My goal is to nudge my readers toward a new window through which to see the human landscape.

UnSpirituality and Permission to Be Human are bold ideas at a time when western metaphysical thought has come to an abrupt reality check in 2012. So many speculations have led up to this moment in time with the anticipation of the end of world events. Predictions were made by metaphysical legends such as Helena Petrovna Blavatsky (1831-1891 - founder of the Theosophists), Edgar Cayce (a famous American psychic) and a long line of spiritual teachers whose failed convictions disappeared in the sunlight of time.

Vague as they were, all prophecies pointed to a time of returning messiahs, alien invasions, landmass upheavals and catastrophic events, such as the pole shift, where some believe the planet will rotate 180 degrees and wipe out all life on Earth. Although geological records show evidence for magnetic pole reversals in the past, our science does not support an eminent doomsday scenario outside the self-destructive tendency of man and womankind.

Many spiritual prophecies about world events have not passed the test of time. The result tells a tale of wishful thinking and presumptuous intuitive leaps. I speculate that persons making such prophecies of doom *may have been perceiving their inner world as such and projected that image and feeling upon their audience.*

I wrote unSpirituality at the end of a 26-year journey. Fueled by childhood trauma, I set out to find answers to my plight. Having been raised in the western orthodox tradition, I was privy to an insider's look at the religious landscape. I later delved into the mysteries of metaphysics and the occult which turned into a daily need-to-know campaign for truth.

What felt like a grueling, never-ending, tromp through the jungles of esoteric thought ended in an unexpected series of realizations. I was sure that my investigation into the sacred teachings would lead me to the ultimate unifying truth. By traversing the valleys of emotional healing, and scaling the mountains of mystical thought, I came to find the answers to the spiritual story not in its confirmation, but it's undoing. Much to my surprise, the Holy Grail was sitting there all the time . . . I had only to look at the obvious.

In this book, I set out to define the spiritual landscape from a fresh point of view, one based on evolution as the primary source for defining our existence. I am no academic on the subject. I share the realizations that the spiritual quest has yielded in my life. I found that understanding our human origins does not require a skilled intellectual; it is a subject simple for the sane and comprehensible to a child. It is, in actuality, built into our biology—we have only to understand who we are.

Throughout this writing, I use the words subjective, religious and spiritual interchangeably. I am at a disadvantage describing what can only be experienced. The word "subjective" is a replacement word for spiritual when it refers to our inner experience. The words 'spiritual and religious' are used to cover metaphysical ideas across the broad landscape of both orthodox and occult systems.

I have done my best to maintain an environment of openness, objectivity and unashamed assertion, so as not to dilute the potency of the message. My hope is to spark new ideas to bridge the emerging dialog on evolution and its relationship to the spiritual tradition. And most earnestly, to introduce the reader to a Bio-Spiritual perspective using a method called Focusing. (focusing.org)

I Am Primate

I was once taught, that I am a soul in a body.
I once believed I was separate from the earth.
A stranger in a strange land,
a sinner in need of a Savior.
But, isn't this my home? This beautiful world?
Isn't this my form?
These hands, these eyes, this touch?
Am I to believe I have violated a rule,
just by being born?
Who claims this right to judge,
and on what authority do you stand?
The truth screams out from my cells.
I am not the imagination of a God,
I am a voice in the earth,
I am that which you deny!
The earth is my home and the stars my destiny.
I will touch the planets through
the hands of my children
. . . not the will of your ghost!
I am a voice in the evolutionary continuum
and I claim the right to be alive,
without your story.
For I Am Human, I Am Proud,
and I AM . . . PRIMATE!

Christopher Loren

Part 1 | **unSpirituality**

Chapter 1

BAMBOOZLED

"Pay no attention to the man behind the curtain!"
— L. Frank Baum

If you are a human being living on earth you have most likely been exposed to spirituality, in its many forms, through personal experience or by association. Even without affiliation, just by being human, you are exposed to an environment peppered with religious symbols, architecture and advertising. From churches, temples and retreats, to the heights of political power where public confessions are made, and oaths are sworn to an invisible force called God. Even our media is filled with personalities who present spiritual ideas mixed with health and psychology. From the obscure to the blatant, other-dimensional ideas exist throughout our world creating a tapestry of paths for personal enrichment and enlightenment. And in the case of religion—obedience!

Unlike religion, however, spirituality blends in with our society in a subtle, yet pervasive way. With spirituality, you can be a Christian, Buddhist, Hindu, Scientologist, Shaman, Psychic, Energy Healer or Massage Therapist because a spiritual being is not dependent on a religion or vocation, rather, it is *having* a human experience, so anyone can join the party. This is a step up from religion because it extends beyond the exclusive belief system of the group into the very fabric of society.

References made by believers, no matter how elementary, tend to refer to something unseen. These can be as simple as "your energy looks great" to "the spirit is guiding me." As innocuous as these statements may appear, spirituality implies an alternate external reality. But I find this assertion limited because it is based on dualism which is the belief in the separation of spirit and matter. It is based on faith in a spiritual story rather than the consilience of psychology, neuroscience and evolution. It hints from obscure belief systems rooted in our mythic past. And because spirituality is subjective and invisible, the unseen quest puts one on a never-ending treadmill in the land of mirrors. In this book I argue that this type of thinking is just another face of the old-time religion.

I spent decades in the religious and metaphysical landscape sampling the abundance of belief systems readily available to the eager seeker. Having been raised a Christian, the spirit-realm was introduced at a very young age. I assumed that a spiritual dimension outside of myself existed and, when I grew into a cognitive adult, I took the Bible at its word and became a missionary and evangelist. But when I put the biblical story to the test through fervent study and application, I ended up departing from the faith. My questions out-matched the confusing answers.

In my quest to understand who I was as a spirit and what my mission was on earth, I turned to the study of metaphysics from both the light and dark schools. Over the course of more than two and a half decades I learned from a variety of teachers who serendipitously graced my path at the right place and time.

Eventually, I came to Sedona, Arizona to be near the cutting edge of spirituality where my quest culminated in a human awakening. This journey is chronicled in my book: unspiritual: A Spiritual Journey. The one thing I found in common from Christianity to metaphysics was the belief in an external dimension called the spirit-realm. This is a world filled with good and bad entities and an all-pervasive awareness called God or Consciousness. But instead of dismissing the supernatural altogether, my search led me to redefining this magical realm from a natural perspective; for I had experienced the mystical in profound, unmistakable ways.

Like opening Pandora's box, my eyes freshly questioned why churches and temples were scattered across continents displaying symbolism that referred to the spirit-realm. Why do people feel the need to call themselves "souls" when their existence as living, breathing, human beings is evident? Why do some humans put more emphasis on the spiritual realm rather than the natural world in which they live? Is it possible that the concept of spirituality could be an addiction to the unseen *because it's unseen?* That the thing we cannot touch drives us crazy? Is the grass *really greener* on the other side of the natural fence?

I believe the answer exists in the misunderstanding of what we call spirit or souls. It began to make more sense to me that spirituality was human produced psycho-emotional energy homegrown from the earth. It was a result of biology and evolution rather than a channeled force from another dimension. I turned my focus toward the ancestral animals from which we evolved as the true source of this fuzzy concept called a soul. It seemed there was little difference between *soul sensing* and *primate sensing*.

I reached a point where I could no longer tolerate the communal denial prevalent in the spiritual community. I refused to swallow the stories of fantastic miracles and supernatural assertions so casually flung around. All these claims reeked of anecdotal evidence and wishful thinking. I concluded that no one had ever shown me a true alteration of the laws of physics. Oh yes, my life was filled with synchronicity and natural miracles were occurring as I recovered and healed the lost parts of my inner world. But there were no physics altering evidence from the so-called new-age magicians who touted the "super" natural in their books and lectures.

All the claims regarding levitation, bilocation and inter-dimensional travel (to name a few) appeared more subjective than actual and gave way to a wide range of interpretation. I mean, if you see a footprint in your front yard just after your guru from India said he visited you through the astral realm, wouldn't it be more interesting if you turned your camera on and asked him to do it again? Of course, it is easy to talk about esoteric feats (pun intended), but much more difficult to deliver the real-time visual evidence. And therefore, the invisible functions just like the imagination. Why not just show people the miracle rather than talk about it?

Validating subjective imaginings through interpersonal relationships seemed to be the function of much of the faith-based spiritual community. However, I am not saying there is no real healing in this arena. I have experienced many transformative moments in the context of subjective fantasies and metaphysical musings which increased my understanding of the inner world, or as I prefer to call it, the Bio-Imagination. This reinterpretation of the inner world is the focus of my philosophy.

I challenged common people and spiritual leaders about their super-natural story. I asked them if they could demonstrate miracles before my eyes, but none could. Instead, I got a set of excuses that reduced the omnipotent spirit down to human time tables. It appears that god or spirit only conducts miracles in certain situations under certain conditions. And most, if not all, miracles appear in the eye of the beholder as from another dimension outside the body, which is of course—invisible. And because it is invisible, who's to tell it is none other than our subjective environment of feelings, memories, images, fears and fantasies we experience in and around our body every waking and sleeping breath.

I also noticed with most people that the imagination was generally experienced somewhere in the head (image), and spirituality (feeling) was felt in and around the body. So, I decided to put them together as one current of energy called the Bio-Imagination. And when I did that, a lot changed. I got more results from my inner work by switching from a dualistic viewpoint of matter and spirit to a bio-spiritual current of energy. What this meant was the entire body was the creator of what spiritualists called auras, the field, channeled energy, etc. This realization brought me to a deeper understanding of the dynamics of our biology and its subjective relationship to nature. Instead of alternate dimensions outside of ourselves how about deeper dimensions within that reveal the treasures of nature? I arrived at the gates of perception holding the keys to the mystical realm we assign to spirit.

> *"The kingdom of heaven is spread upon on the earth and men do not see it"*
>
> - Gospel of Thomas 113

If you have felt something fishy might be going on with the spirit-realm or have arrived at a place where you are sincerely questioning your spiritual experiences, then this book is for you. It took me decades to consider the question "have I been bamboozled?" Is it imaginable that all this matter and spirit dualism is a cultural hangover from our superstitious past? Could it be that the archetypes and inner self reflections are no different than the gods, demons and spirits that some believe are real? Is it possible that human biology *is* the creator of spirituality and the natural world its playground of perception? Is the real reason why the answers to our questions act more like a carrot on a stick than a satisfying meal because we are looking in the wrong direction?

I concluded that human primates are ghost makers, phantom producers, magicians on the highest level able to fool even themselves with their own magic and even create self-inflicted booby traps they can't unlock.

When I started entertaining these thoughts, I was led down the road of scientific research and deeper occult studies. For the first time, I set my eyes on the sciences around evolution. Rather than trying to validate the spirit-realm, I challenged every claim I could find. What I discovered, while the little dog called "curiosity" pulled away the curtain, was the human primate behind the Great and Powerful Oz.[1]

I found a consistency in my new line of study that led to the natural world as an explanation for what we have traditionally assigned to the "super" natural. Spirituality made more sense in the context of feelings and imagination within a virtual bio-world than the stories of reincarnated souls and afterlives.

It occurred to me how important it was that our internal world be approached from a place of curiosity and wonderment as a living-informative-process. An environment that is taken seriously as a bio-spiritual ecosystem. Where the language of archetypes and the movement of energy is understood like music and art with the full spectrum of sound and color. And where its reflective nature is as clear as a reflection on water.

The soul-body split also sheds light on a well-known phenomenon called *cognitive dissonance* which is the feeling of discomfort one gets while holding two opposing beliefs at the same time "I am a human but I'm not *really* human, I am a soul." I assert that this soul emerges from our biology and that we truly are bio-spiritual animals.

> *"One of the saddest lessons of history is this: If we've been bamboozled long enough, we tend to reject any evidence of the bamboozle. We're no longer interested in finding out the truth. The bamboozle has captured us. It's simply too painful to acknowledge, even to ourselves, that we've been taken. Once you give a charlatan power over you, you almost never get it back."*
> — Carl Sagan

Chapter 2

DEFINING SPIRITUALITY

*"Spiritual life is the bouquet of natural life,
not a supernatural thing imposed upon it."*
— Joseph Campbell

The term 'spirituality' covers a vast landscape of partitioned beliefs from the Egyptians and Gnostics to today's evangelical movement and quantum consciousness. The word has implied different things to various cultures throughout history. In its secular version, it is related to words such as love, patience, contentment, harmony, concern for others and altruism, all of which reflect the best in Homo sapiens. In the religious sense, however, the meaning of spirituality jumps off into the *super*-natural. Here we find a departure from the natural world into a mystical unseen realm.

The spiritual landscape is a world of invisibility where mysterious beings operate in hidden realms. Some systems of belief describe a hierarchical order where God is at the helm of a structured cosmology while others convey a pantheon of higher beings complete with time loops, dimensions and alternate universes. A chronology of the history of spirituality would take up volumes, but for the subject at hand, I will list a short progression, to put in perspective how the word has evolved.

In the 5th century, at the end of the middle ages, words translatable as spirituality began to surface and make their way into the common vocabulary. The term represented heretical ideas outside the religious tradition which placed innovators at risk of losing their reputations and lives. In the 18th century, thinkers opposed to religion translated its meaning into a more sublime expression of emotion.

Ralph Waldo Emerson put the word on the map in his Transcendentalist movement as "an intuitive experience." Transcendentalism suggested that we could intuit truth through our communion with nature rather through an edict from God.

In modern times, the current version of spirituality is termed "Consciousness." It is an all-encompassing name which includes everyone and everything in the cosmos rather than a chosen few. Being 'spiritual rather than religious' is vogue and shielded from the typical orthodox ridicule and bias. Spirituality, from this perspective, allows for more articulate explanations. Serve up a bowl of Quantum Physics and the Holographic Theory, throw in a dash of "What the Bleep Do We Know,"[1] and you have a delicious buffet of paradigms.

Let's look at the description of spirituality from Merriam-Webster:

1. The quality or fact of being spiritual.
2. Incorporeal or immaterial nature.
3. Predominantly spiritual character as shown in thought, life, etc.
4. Property or revenue of the church or of an ecclesiastic in his or her official capacity.[2]

Spirituality is the concept of an alleged immaterial reality, it points to existence beyond the natural world. Even so, this word has evolved over time and now refers to our Subjective reality in more general terms. Let's look at a few more definitions:

> An inner path enabling a person to discover the essence of his or her being; or the "deepest values and meanings by which people live."[3]
>
> Spiritual practices, including meditation, prayer and contemplation, are intended to develop an individual's inner life. Transcendent experiences can include being connected to a larger reality, yielding a more comprehensive self, joining with other individuals or the human community, with nature or the cosmos, or with the divine realm.[4]
>
> Spirituality is often experienced as a source of inspiration or orientation in life.[5]
>
> Spirituality encompasses a belief in immaterial realities or experiences of the transcendent nature of the world.[6]

All these definitions sound meaningful and fantastic, but does the word really imply metaphysical? The etymology (root definition) of the English word "spirit" is the Latin word *spiritus* which means "soul, courage or breath." *Spiritus* replaced the classical Latin version *animus* which was derived from the Indo-European root meaning "to breathe."[7]

The word "breath" is an Old English word meaning "air exhaled from lungs." As you can see, it is a natural definition. If one were religious, speculations could arise to support the belief that air is a product of the supernatural. This word, however, is not characterized as anything esoteric in its base definition. It appears that the earliest definitions infer a much less "spiritual" meaning than how it is understood today.

Throughout the ancient world the soul was treated as part of the body. It was no different than breath or wind. Victor Stenger, professor of physics and astronomy at the University of Hawaii, states in his book, *The New Atheism*:

> The Hebrew word for soul is *nephish*, which is translated as "life" and connected to breathing. Also in Hebrew, *ruah* is translated as "wind" or "breath," and sometimes "spirit," "soul," "life" or "consciousness."
>
> The association of the soul or life force with breath also occurred in the isolated Hawaiian Islands. According to one undocumented story from an oral culture, in old Hawaii, when someone died, native shamans tried to breathe life back into the body by shouting, "Ha!" in the body's face. When Western doctors came to Hawaii and were observed not to do this, they were called "Ha-ole," which meant "without breath." To this day whites are called "Haoles" in Hawaii.
>
> So, for most of the history, the soul was considered part of the body—as material as wind. The ancient atomists assumed the soul was made of atoms just like everything else. And Christianity maintained a unity of body and soul, with Jesus being fully resurrected in the body.[8]

It appears that there is a significant focus on the physical process of breathing. Spirituality has acquired diverse and sometimes conflicting meanings, so, without going into a myriad of explanations, I will proceed with the root definition as a template from which to work. In its immediate definition, the word implies physical properties, so how does the word find its place in the non-physical arena? Simply put—death!

The earliest evidence of religious thought is founded on the ritual treatment of the dead. The relics of ritual burials tell a tale of man's early awareness of life and death. For the rest of the animal kingdom death is a relatively normal event. In the case of our ancestors, the ability to self-reflect upon the natural world was expressed through art and ritual. With the onset of language and symbol mankind began to conceptualize the environment. Behavioral Neuroscientist Todd Murphy explains:

> At this point in our evolutionary history, a fundamentally new experience became possible. A person could look at a dead body, remember the experience, think about it, personalize the whole thing, and conclude that the same thing is going to happen to them. Language skills are utilized, and the sentence appears in the mind: "I will die." The conclusion is reached without the person having any first-hand experience at all.[9]

This development was a cornerstone in the evolution of our brain.

> When we first appeared as a species, our brains expanded in two important areas: the frontal lobes, which have to do with planning, anticipating things, and projecting into the future, and the temporal lobes, which have to do with memory. Both large areas have many other functions, but these two stand out when we are talking about understanding death. The temporal lobes

> expanded, and now included language comprehension areas, and the frontal lobes grew to include language production areas. The human sense of self changed to include a component that dealt in language, so that we began to take words personally, and to feel our "selves" affected by what others say to us.[9]

Our ability to create a concept not only affected the way we interpreted other humans, but it also changed the way we looked at death and rebirth. He continues:

> The concept is very threatening. Our new cognitive skills would allow a lot more imagination than before, and it would have been very adaptive for us to use this skill to imagine as many ways of dying as possible. The more ways of dying we can imagine, the more ways we can avoid. But death anxiety is very stressful. If we were aware of our death at all times, we would be at risk for several psychoses, like the ones that follow the development of the normally fear-laden temporal lobe seizures. Persinger has theorized that we developed a mechanism that shuts death anxiety off—the spiritual experience.[9]

The word, spirituality, takes on a fresh new light when viewed from an evolutionary standpoint. The spiritual concept was born and mythologies developed labeling the natural world with our ideas, fears and fantasies. Spirituality has a physical reference as well as a conceptual one. It is in the conceptualization of nature that our species has fallen into a trap. As harmless as this may appear, there lays a hidden culprit within this narrative on which I will elaborate in the following chapters.

Replacing spiritual terminology with "human Subjective experience" grants a more honest appraisal of the phenomenon at hand. The word "Subjective" is described in the dictionary as "existing in the mind; belonging to the thinking subject rather than to the object of thought."[10] This distinction is so important that I cannot stress it enough. Our memories, feelings and beliefs are the lens through which we see the world. If we believe our Subjective perceptions without question, we become susceptible to delusions. If we understand how our emotions communicate through archetypes and symbolism (like dreams), we can learn a new subjective/biological language.

I believe critical thinking skills are essential for integrating our Subjective experience with the outer world which removes the dependency on the shaman, pastor or god. We are literally looking through a Subjective window into our experience of the universe. It is of utmost importance to develop a relationship with the inner aspects of ourselves in order to relate to the universe around us. Humans are literally "seeing" through their thoughts and feelings.

Spirituality covers a broad spectrum of meanings in our culture, but ultimately it is a concept that points to the Subjective human experience from which our myths, stories and fantasies are born.

Chapter 3

THE NEVER ENDING STORY

"Belief is the death of intelligence."
— Robert Anton Wilson

"When enough insane people scream in harmony that they really are healthy, they can actually start to believe themselves. Or put even more simply: people with overlapping delusions get along wonderfully."
— Daniel Mackler

There would be no spirituality without a story. Whether you believe in consciousness as a "Universal Force" or you hold on to more traditional beliefs where an ancient figure is revered, there is always a narrative to support the invisible world.

I find it interesting that the spiritual story requires a tale of grandiose proportions. It is just not good enough to simply be human. The unseen story is so vital to the religious mind that life without it appears hopeless and bleak. I wondered about this for years, why do we need a spiritual story? Why do we need a god or goddess? Is not life in all its tangible and Subjective glory, enough?

The reason lies in our ancient past. It appears that mythology served to free us from the hard realities of the natural world. Feelings such as fear, vulnerability, weakness and loss were relieved by the belief in the *super*-natural. The feeling of "irrational control" was born and the addiction to the invisible made its way into the fiber of the human primate. As the mythological story evolved, new stories arose among cultures, maintaining common symbolic forms (based in nature), but differing in environmental expression.

The spiritual story created a refuge for the fearful primates. The holy temple of god, prayer and petition became the safe house for the uncertain. The spiritual became the real and the natural world the unreal. An everlasting incorporeal self was born in this unknown invisible land where one could defy all natural laws simply by associating themselves with the spiritual world. This brand new "inner person" was immune to the dictates of the flesh and the demands of the material world, and because this idea offered ultimate freedom, it became the drug of choice for evolving primates. The natural landscape became a canvas for this imagined scheme; churches and temples were built, sacred places and megalithic monuments were erected, and the metaphysical landscape became a reality for our species.

From tooth and claw to Facebook, our perception of the world changed over time. Without these stories, our species might have never beaten the environmental factors they were up against. The problem is that most of humanity is still attached to the spiritual story like a baby to a bottle—we forgot it was all imagined.

Move forward to present time and look around. We are living in a world where people still believe they are invisible beings. Churches abound in every town and city and spirituality has become a household word. Television is filled with examples of people thanking god for their successes while world hunger devours the prayers of the suffering.

Let's take a closer look at the spiritual story through one of the early doctrines—Spiritism.

In the 19th century, French educator Allan Kardec compiled the doctrine of Spiritism as a system of explanations for the supernatural phenomenon. Spiritist Codification was the name given for the five books that comprised a philosophy based on life after death and the existence of Spirits.

The main principles of Spiritism are as follows:

- God is the Supreme Intelligence—First Cause of all things.

- God is eternal, immutable, immaterial, unique, all powerful, sovereignty, just and good.

- A Spirit is not an abstract, undefined being, only to be conceived of by our thought; it is a real, circumscribed being, which, in certain cases, is appreciable by the senses of sight, hearing, and touch.

- All Spirits are destined to attain perfection by passing through the different degrees of the Spirit-hierarchy. This amelioration is affected by incarnation, which is imposed on some of them as expiation, and on others as a mission. Material life is a trial which they have to undergo many times until they have attained to absolute perfection.

- A Spirit's successive corporeal existences are always progressive, and never retrograde; but the rapidity of our progress depends on the efforts we make to arrive at the perfection.

- The soul possessed its own individuality before its incarnation; it preserves that individuality after its separation from the body.

- On its re-entrance into the Spirit world, the soul again finds there all those whom it has known upon the earth, and all its former existences eventually come back to its memory, with the remembrance of all the good and of all the evil which it has done in them.

- Spirits exert an incessant action upon the moral world, and even upon the physical world; they act both upon matter and upon thought, and constitute one of the powers of nature, the efficient cause of many classes of phenomena hitherto unexplained or misinterpreted.

- Spirits are incessantly in relation with men. The good Spirits try to lead us into the right road, sustain us under the trials of life, and aid us to bear them with courage and resignation; the bad ones tempt us to evil: it is a pleasure for them to see us fall, and to make us like themselves.

- The moral teaching of the higher Spirits may be summed up, like that of Christ, in the gospel maxim, 'Do unto others as you would that others should do unto you;' that is to say, do good to all, and wrong no one. This principle of action furnishes mankind with a rule of conduct of universal application, from the smallest matters to the greatest.[1]

In the above description, we find a list of assertions that have no basis in the physical world. From time immemorial, the story of invisibility has had its main character "God" and its cast of "Spirits" in the invisible realm. No one to date has been able to prove that any of this really exists, yet, the belief in the incorporeal continues.

In the Christian story, Adam and Eve disobeyed the supreme invisible ruler and we, their progenies, inherited their sinful nature. Fortunately, (lucky us) God (aka-Jehovah) devised a plan to make up for mankind's inherited sins by sending a perfect sacrifice to appease his wrath. Once the "sent one" rose from the dead, he promised to return and "save" earthlings from an even bigger judgment reserved for those who reject God's little deal—accept my human sacrifice or die!

Notice that every aspect of this story is founded in the invisible. Christians like to argue for the historical case of Christ's crucifixion, but there is little evidence it ever happened. Read *"The Christ Conspiracy: The Greatest Story Ever Sold"* by Acharya S. Page.

In the spiritual story, there is a chronicle of life before birth, life after death and the spiritual being having a human experience that is undertaken by "choice" from the other world. Believers assert that all events happen as lessons they agreed to undergo. The physical properties of evolution are ignored, and the obsession with the afterlife continues, along with a myriad of speculations. I included the main principles of Spiritism to paint a picture of the spiritual landscape. These beliefs might appear insane to some, yet, even so, a cultural certainty in these beliefs persists and the effect on our maturity is taking its toll.

Even in the face of evolving sciences the belief in the supernatural strives to gain precedence over the facts of the natural world. Scientific models such as string theory, quantum gravity, particle physics and the holographic principle present impressive theories about how our universe works. But, whereas science willingly assigns skepticism to its theories, the spiritual mind scrapes the crumbs off the floor of scientific research and runs eagerly to impress the locals.

In some instances, scientific research is sadly misrepresented, such as the case of author Deepak Chopra, who, in a debate with scientists Sam Harris and Michael Shermer took the term "non-locality" out of context in an effort to support his metaphysical poetry.[2] The grasping of quantum physics is not an easy task and I find it less than useful to toss misunderstood scraps to a trusting audience. I prefer to believe in the good intentions of Mr. Chopra however misleading his words were in this debate. This is nothing new. Throughout history, believers have either fought against regulated inquiry or attempted to distort it.

Neuroscientist Sam Harris expands on the idea:

> There is simply no question that people have transformative experiences as a result of engaging contemplative disciplines like meditation, and there is no question that these experiences shed some light on the nature of the human mind (any experience does for that matter). What is highly questionable are the metaphysical claims that people make based on these experiences. I do not make such claims.

Nor do I support the metaphysical claims of others.[4]

Another example of this dichotomy is the movie "What the *Bleep* Do We Know." David Albert, a philosopher of physics, stated during an interview that the film makers took his comments out of context to make it appear as though he endorsed the film's thesis. Dr. Albert stated that he *was "profoundly unsympathetic to attempts at linking quantum mechanics with consciousness."*[5] I would agree that this movie opened the minds of millions to an expanded and fruitful vision of the universe, and I think, for the most part, it did a lot of good. However, *radical curiosity* (my term for real-time intelligent inquiry) should challenge any scientific claims, for inaccurate or misleading information, especially when these claims are implying metaphysical realities. If a thing is true, it will stand the test of critical inquiry.

Victor Stenger explains what he calls the "myth of Quantum Consciousness:"

> The myth of quantum consciousness sits well with many whose egos have made it impossible for them to accept the insignificant place science perceives for humanity, as modern instruments probe the farthest reaches of space and time. Quantum consciousness has about as much substance as the aether from which it is composed. Early in this century, quantum mechanics and Einstein's relativity destroyed the notion of a holistic universe that had seemed within the realm of possibility in the century just past. First, Einstein did away with the aether,

> shattering the doctrine that we all move about inside a universal, cosmic fluid whose excitations connect us simultaneously to one another and to the rest of the universe. Second, Einstein and other physicists proved that matter and light were composed of particles, wiping away the notion of universal continuity. Atomic theory and quantum mechanics demonstrated that everything, even space and time, exists in discrete bits – quanta. To turn this around and say that twentieth-century physics initiated some new holistic view of the universe is a complete misrepresentation of what actually took place. The myth of quantum consciousness should take its place along with Gods, unicorns, and dragons as yet another product of the fantasies of people unwilling to accept what science, reason, and their own eyes tell them about the world.[6]

These few examples highlight the strong disagreement leading scientists have with the metaphysical claims made by spiritualists. My purpose is not to elaborate on this debate, but to establish that a dilemma exists, in that the spiritualists attempt to certify their claims by leaping to extrapolated conclusions. Research regarding the body as a source of innate wisdom, is, in my opinion, worthy of notice. Millions of years of evolutionary wisdoms lives within each one of us just waiting to be tapped.

It is obvious to a reasonable mind that our planet is not a mere 6,000 years old. The evidence suggest that it is well over 4 billion years old. Nevertheless, the religious mind continues to insist on the former, based solely on the bible, even in the face of raw geological data. The same irrationality is applied to the belief in reincarnation. Although the evidence for reincarnation is speculative (in my opinion the phenomenon points to genetic memory. Consider the possibility of two people struck with the feeling of "soul mate" actually having the same ancestors "in love" at some point down the corridors of their genetic tree), there remains a battle for the soul in spite of evidence for our evolutionary roots.

Buddha himself made references in doubt of the phantom phenomenon.[7]

> As there is no self, there is no transmigration of self; but there are deeds and continued effects of deeds. These deeds are being done, but there is no doer. There is no entity that migrates, no self is transferred from one place to another; but there is a voice uttered here and the echo comes back.

These examples do not invalidate the "experience" of spirituality. Rather, they suggest that humans are still defining transcendental experiences from an out dated perspective. Modern brain and neurological research have traced mystical experiences to the functions of the brain and nervous system.

Researchers Stanley Koren and Michael Persinger conducted experiments with a device called the "God Helmet." The device produces magnetic fields that induce the feeling of the presence of God. Subjects describe sensing "presences" that they interpret as departed loved ones, angels, or other beings and speak of out-of-body experiences and altered states. The fact that this device can turn on and off mystical experiences suggests locality of the phenomenon to the human organism rather than a mysterious force.[8]

Neuroscientist V.S. Ramachandran conducted research on the Phantom Limb Syndrome. His research shows that the experience of the phantom limb is created by a wide network of interconnected neural structures; the sensations of pain are found to be located in the brain via the visual centers. Evidence for phantom limbs being anything astral or spiritual does not appear. Ramachandran demonstrated his theory by showing that stroking distinct parts of his patient's face led to perceptions of being touched on distinctive parts of the missing limb which links the physical connection to the felt phenomenon.

Another aspect of his research connects patients with spiritual inclinations to temporal lobe seizures. There is much to explore in this area which makes a compelling case for the body as the source of transcendental experiences.[9]

The descriptions of the unseen are as varied as the persons questioned. Versions of the incorporeal narrative change as if being reworked in a human editing room depending on the teacher, book or guru, relevant at the time. If the information was coming from an outside source, one would think that at the least, there should be some consistency in the interpretation of the unseen that would set it apart from the natural world. The obvious constant is, *the human body produces repeatable Subjective phenomenon in present time in the form of feelings, emotions and images, and it is these that are projected onto the landscape of the world.*

One of the dangers of the spiritual story is that it disassociates humans from reality. Relieving world hunger, crime and suffering are replaced with fantasies of other worlds, dimensions, gods or forces that will magically take care of humanities plight. I once asked a metaphysical friend of mine what she thought of rape. She replied, "People choose these experiences before birth to learn human lessons of rape." I asked her about world hunger, sex trafficking, genocide, and torture, and she replied with the same logic. At that moment, I realized the dangerous implications of esoteric ideology in our world.

Separating one's "self" physically from the world (as an unseen entity) alienates the human being from the facts of a sensual world and its realities. To have a self, you must provide a story for that self. Whether it is the tale of past pain or future fears the etheric self requires a story because it is hitchhiking on the natural. The natural world is covered over by this ghostly film. The incorporeal image, fueled by the forces of the body, must feed, and, in its empiric way, usurp the authority of its host. This denial grants a "way out" of the human condition, and yet, it is only through our acceptance that we can we reverse the tide.

Metaphysical belief systems create the illusion of a causal divine agent who will fix the world's problems, which in turn, *justifies inaction for the believer*. A good example of this sort of cognitive dissonance is in India where gurus are revered as "loving" beings while the country is plagued with poverty. How can a population whose majority (80%) accepts reincarnation as a tenant of their faith allow the poor to be victimized to such a degree? Who's creating "that" reality?

> "There is no society in human history that ever suffered because its people became too reasonable."
> — Sam Harris

Although many religions have a history of feeding the hungry and clothing the poor, this is always done "in the name" of their religion of choice. Thus, the disassociation continues to spread, linking the invisible agent with basic human needs. Humanitarian aid is not a function of the unseen, but a duty of our species.

The spiritual story has missed the boat. I prefer to think that we are life consciously evolving as the human experience. When I think of the millions of years of evolution and the natural organic process by which we became human, I get excited. When I look at the intelligence and depth of feeling, the intuitive inner gut and peripheral sensitivity that some call psychic—I am in awe. Because it took life so very, very long to develop this perennial wisdom, it is not difficult to assume that evolution dwarfs the spiritual story and celebrates the inner life of the human being.

Overall, the spiritual story is an age-old religious theme updated into a quasi-world of unfounded assertions. This never-ending story changes shape with the times, holding irrational dreams and nightmares like a carrot on a stick. Like a virus, it spreads from person to person invalidating the natural world we live in—a world with real problems and earned dreams.

Chapter 4

THE INVISIBLE SELF

"The soul looks just as it should look if it doesn't exist"
— Victor Stenger

"I cannot imagine a God who rewards and punishes the objects of his creation, whose purposes are modeled after our own - a God, in short, who is, but a reflection of human frailty. Neither can I believe that the individual survives the death of his body, although feeble souls harbor such thoughts through fear or ridiculous egotism."
— Albert Einstein

"All I say is that I think it is damned unlikely that anything like a central cosmic will, a Spirit world, or an eternal survival of personality exist. They are the most preposterous and unjustified of all the guesses which can be made about the universe, and I am not enough of a hair-splitter to pretend that I don't regard them as arrant and negligible moonshine. In theory I am an agnostic, but pending the appearance of radical evidence I must be classed, practically and provisionally, as an atheist."
— H.P. Lovecraft

Spirituality conjures thoughts of realities beyond the human experience. However, there is a shorter version of the word that implies *identity* and that is "spirit." Aside from the former's generalities, the word, spirit, carries a strong and specific implication—*you are a spirit.*

Implying that a person is a spirit disassociates them from being human. Graciously, from this perspective, the body is given titles such as "sacred," "temple" or "vehicle." As holy and generous as these descriptions might sound, *they objectify the body placing it in a subordinate position to the assumed invisible entity.*

How did this come about? Where did we get the idea that the physical body was somehow subordinate to this invisible being? How did we come to have a self-concept? The word "self" comes from the root words "separate and apart." The spiritual tradition splits the concept of "self" into two groups: 1) the self as ego or superficial self of the body and mind, sometimes referred to as the "false self," and 2) the self who is named as "the witness," "the observer" or "the higher self." There is a higher self and a lower self.

The concept of self, whether it is a positive or negative one, develops early in a human life. The acts of primary caregivers and environmental anomalies imprint emotionally potent images deep within the young organism. From feelings and imagination to sticks and stones, the child's experience gathers a timeline of memories that can enforce a toxic conceptual image (positive or negative) or enhance their natural maturation, hopefully, unsullied by compulsive identification.

Children from families that naturally demonstrate love, communication and caring don't typically struggle with the severity of conflict that occurs in a traumatic upbringing. The child whose imagination has been nurtured is more likely to mature into a creative and productive adult. On the other hand, with traumatic rearing, the imagination freezes into emotionally charged memories/identities that create conflict with the human organism and its environment. Physical abuse, coupled with beliefs that contradict reality (religious ideology-dualism), polarizes the child into an inner world of conflict in order to protect them from the perceived world "out there."

The word "trauma" may invoke only images of *physical* abuse because the Subjective offense is easy to overlook. In the case of religion, teaching a child biblical stories might seem innocent, but in fact, one is teaching a dark fantasy rather than reality. It might appear harmless, but when these stories are reinforced by the belief and emotional charge of the parents, a child has no choice, but to adopt irrational ideas about life—thus imprinting the dualistic concept which is in disagreement with the natural world.

A self-concept can be useful in a person's life or it can be a handicap depending on their treatment and training. If one has a good understanding of their life experience and are not plagued with self-depreciating memories or grandiose images of self, they can get on learning and growing and developing naturally. On the other hand, a person who has been forced to identify with the content of their imagination is stuck in a vicious loop that reinforces the image they have become. The need to validate this reflection arises *because* it is a fantasy, a mirage, and because it is fueled by the organism, it must feed to stay alive. It is akin to being trapped in a mirror of one's own creation.

In the book "Trapped in the Mirror," Elan Golomb writes:

> People who are free of narcissistic traits (most of us have some) do not attempt to place themselves above others. They are unconcerned with such comparisons. They stay in touch with their feelings and try to do their personal best. Their standards are internal and realistic since they have a good

> idea of who they are and what they can accomplish. They are free of idealistic wishes and dreams.
>
> Narcissists are wholly different. They unconsciously deny an unstated, and intolerably poor, self-image through inflation. They turn themselves into glittering figures of immense grandeur surrounded by psychologically impenetrable walls. The goal of this self-deception is to be impervious to greatly feared external criticism and to their own roiling sea of doubts.[1]

The subject of narcissism is commonly viewed as the plight of one who is in love with an inflated image of self. Often it is the case of the male who has an ego the size of New York and a lifestyle to match. The same projection of grandiosity applies to spirituality.

Why would a living breathing natural person deny their humanity and replace it with an invisible entity? What's the catch? What makes being human so insufficient that a spirit should take its place? I believe the answer lies in the centuries of god-fearing, esoteric-bowing programming that our species has inherited. Modern spirituality is just a kinder and gentler version of the theological and philosophical split created by dualism.

> Dissociation (being split-off from one's deepest truth) mimics enlightenment—but it isn't enlightenment. People who are dissociated live in great peace. But this is only because they have blocked their negative feelings. The enlightened person

> resolves his negatives feelings, and thus his
> peace is not false. — Daniel Mackler

Rene Descartes, a French philosopher (1596-1650), developed the idea of "Cartesian Dualism." It states that there is a mechanical material body and an immaterial soul that interact with each other; the soul acts as the "ghost in the machine," implying superiority over the body. I find it telling that this idea was in response to Thomas Hobbes's (1588-1679) assertion that "all of human experience comes from biological processes contained within the body."

From ancient Zen Buddhism to early 20th century psychology, dualism has flourished. The vast philosophies of the mind that grew out of this ideology spread like wildfire throughout the last century fueling spin-off religions such as Scientology, Science of Mind, Theosophy and Americanized Eastern Mysticism.

In 1971 the dualistic idea grew to epic proportions when Robert Monroe published "Journeys Out of the Body."[2] He coined the name OBE or "out-of-body-experience" and achieved worldwide recognition as an explorer of consciousness which inspired many others to begin writing and reporting on the subject.

Having personally braved a lifetime of out-of-body-experiences, I became familiar with this alleged "spiritual realm." Thanks to the consistency of these nocturnal surprises I had plenty of chances to tinker with the phenomenon. What began as recurring dreams turned into tactile environments through which I could navigate with all of my senses experiencing myself fully awake in the dreamscape.

For decades, I questioned the validity of the experience, trying to put to rest my nagging doubts. I read most of the books on the topic but could never quell the unsettled feeling—the splinter in my mind. I wanted to know if I was literally leaving my body. The dream experiences seemed as real as the waking world and the popular teachers on the subject were raving about surfing the nocturnal waves, yet, things still did not add up.

If I was out of my body and awake in my room then why did the environment change in appearance while other parts remained the same? Most of the room was accurate while other areas extended into a bowling alley or the living room in my childhood home—the logistics did not add up. How could I be certain that this was not an illusion? If the "fleshy" body is used as a reference during spiritual travels, then the physical environment should be held to the same standard.

It wasn't until I discovered a book entitled "The Ego Tunnel" by Thomas Metzinger[3] that my long-awaited answer to the riddle came through. Metzinger, who is himself an astral traveler and cognitive scientist, argues that the "self" is a phenomenon of our biology. The environment that this *self* is navigating in is a simulation *of* our subjective environment. In other words, our conceptual self-image has a world in which it experiences itself and that world is a virtual construct created by the human organism. I knew I had found the long-awaited answer to my nagging suspicions.

I concluded that other dimensions, invisible landscapes and spirit beings were nothing more than Subjective delusions born from the creative imagination. I admit, however, that there are OBE cases that have not been fully explained, but I suspect that biology will continue to answer the questions in this arena.

There is much that we primates are unaware of especially when it comes to the processes in our bodies that create the delusions we believe are real. Add to that, we are composite beings who are connected to a vastly bigger picture than our "little me" might lead us to know. Consider the billions of processes that are at play in our body while dreaming your biggest dream or obsessing over your worst nightmare scenario. This ability would not be possible without the entire biological organism operating as it does, yet, we attribute it to an invisible self, God, force, or little person looking out of the eyes with a first and last name.

Let me make this radiantly clear—*if you believe in spirits and the metaphysical world, your biology will create the illusion that these things are real.* For example, when you decide to buy a car you will see this car everywhere you go. If you have superstitious inclinations, you might assign agency to this event and think "spirit is manifesting my car everywhere." Our internal imagery can just as easily be interpreted as the subjective art that gives our lives meaning.

The subtle events in our lives (such as the cat's meow in the midnight hour) can take on a whole new intensity depending on our belief system. Is the cat simply meowing or is it a sign of dark forces at work? Is the cat's meow music to your ears or does it send a shrill up your spine? Now, does all of this mean that our interpretations are useless? It does not, but it does reveal our evolutionary inclination to place meaning on the patterns in our environment—this phenomenon is called Patternicity.[4]

Patternicity is a term coined by Michael Shermer who is a scientist and the founder of the Skeptics Society. The meaning of patternicity is, *"the tendency in humans to find patterns where there are none."* It is a favored evolutionary trait because it protects us from real threats by recognizing patterns that could be harmful to our survival. The movement in the shrub, the blowing wind, the scent of another animal and the sound of a subtle growl, together, created a survival pattern for our primate ancestors.

Although patternicity has been useful to us it can also work against us because we tend to see patterns through the lens of our delusions and when it comes to spirituality we see patterns *everywhere*. The problem is that believers leap to erroneous conclusions about these patterns without understanding their evolutionary origins. The spiritual self, fuels the seeking of patterns to validate its existence. Understanding this trait is *extremely* helpful in seeing the difference between reality and delusion.

Becoming familiar with patternicity changed the way I process information and helped me decipher truth from fiction in my inquiry process. Intelligent inquiry does not imply having a closed mind, rather, *it is the skillful use of an open mind*. Through the process of inquiry, I stopped believing in unfounded claims. It is easy to be lured into believing our illusions because of our biological need to be certain, but when it comes to religion and spirituality, the landscape is littered with false claims and crushed hopes.

I no longer make the mistake of putting my faith in the paranormal. If evidence for the validity of supernatural claims are produced I will happily embrace new discoveries, but until then (and I'm not holding my breath), I am too busy being in awe of the physical universe, our evolutionary origins and the always present wisdom and guidance of our *biological subjective universe*—which *is* what spirituality has always been pointing to.

Whether a person believes in a spiritual self or not, the ability to experience a deeply felt, rich Subjective life, is available to every human being. It is through the window of our inner environment that we perceive our universe and world. Our feelings are the key to unlocking the treasures that await the courageous.

Part 2 | **The Subjective**

Chapter 5

IMAGINATION

"There came to that room wild streams of violet midnight glittering with dust of gold, vortices of dust and fire, swirling out of the ultimate spaces and heavy perfumes from beyond the worlds. Opiate oceans poured there, litten by suns that the eye may never behold and having in their whirlpools strange dolphins and sea-nymphs of unrememberable depths. Noiseless infinity eddied around the dreamer and wafted him away without touching the body that leaned stiffly from the lonely window; and for days not counted in men's calendars the tides of far spheres that bore him gently to join the course of other cycles that tenderly left him sleeping on a green sunrise shore, a green shore fragrant with lotus blossoms and starred by red camalotes."
— H.P. Lovecraft

"Imagination is the golden-eyed monster that never sleeps. It must be fed; it cannot be ignored."
— Patricia A. McKillip

Imagination is the term we use for internal images and sensations in the human organism. These morphing archetypes provide meaning to our life experience and play a primary role in our development. Imagination is so significant that its very suppression can deform the maturation process. From imaginary friends to fairy tales, a child's world is full of wonder. Take that away, and you have a dark and lonely universe. Like plants and other life forms, human beings grow organically, each stage builds to the next, culminating in a fully bloomed creative adult.

Imagination plays a tricky role with spiritual beliefs because the tendency to identify with the video screen in our heads, which is felt in our nervous system, is so great. It is not common for believers in the supernatural to have a working knowledge of brain science or evolution, therefore, there is no backdrop to compare their imaginings.

The metaphysical tradition teaches that we use our imagination to create our reality, but it is not clear about where the imagination stops, and spiritual dimensions start. I just assumed, having been taught dualism from birth, with no scientific education, that supernatural assertions based on questionable science were true. But how do we define what is real? What criteria do we use to measure reality? Are we to believe that anyone's Subjective fantasies are to be taken seriously? And which one in the tribe gets the final word? Every person's internal world is as different as their thumbprint so how is it possible to define our reality based on the Subjective alone?

The obvious answer is our shared natural existence. Beyond our ever-changing imagination we have the constants shared by every human being on earth—biology and environment. All humans have a brain, and without one, there is no imagination; there is no way to prove that the imagination exists without using the brain. It appears that the imagination is a full body experience, for we are indeed organic dreaming machines.

Children instinctively create imaginary friends. It is something that is nurturing to their development. It is so significant, that its very negation or invalidation by parents can lead to emotional and psychological distress. It appears that the imaginary friend acts as a Subjective projection that informs their experience. If a child is shamed for their intuitive creations or is forced to drop their unseen informant prematurely, an obsession with the invisible may occur. This "letting go" is vital for the development of their self-determinism. It is their creation, so it is their right and duty to assimilate the wisdom of the phantom and release the fantasy when the time has come. I believe this is a key event in the time line of a maturing human.

The inner imaginary universe of the human primate is the battlefield of the ages. Even today, with all the research available on the brain and nervous system, parents re-create the toxic nightmare of their past through authoritarian discipline, shaming, punishing and invalidating out of ignorance and convenience. Can you remember day-dreaming as a child, looking out the window or up in the sky, pondering the wonders of your existence? Do you recall the curious learning process before the pressures of the educational system? It was wonderful, free and natural. So, what happened? What turns a playful, creative child into an emotionally frozen adult?

Like other mammals, humans are innately creative creatures. We have a firm tendency to assert our will, and define ourselves, from a very young age. If a parent is suffering from the plight of dualism, especially if induced through trauma and/or religious teaching, the likelihood of psychological and emotional child abuse is there. The parent's invisible self, threatened by the native impulses of the innocent, seeks to break the will of the young organism. This is done by invalidating and shaming its prey. Adult primates, trapped in the mirror of their own creation, squash the child's spontaneity and wonderment to relieve the tension of their own self-betrayal.

Children say "no" when they are defining their "primate self" apart from other primates. They are discovering the *space* between the two, the power to start and stop, how to define their own will against another, all under the safe and watchful care of their parents. Unfortunately, some parents tend to take this "no" event as a personal attack, a challenge to their authority, or as a demonstration of rebellion from the sinful animal nature. This, I argue, is not a natural response, but the knee-jerk reaction of that which is threatened by the biology—the phantom self, or to put it another way—*fear*. Therefore, the *will* behind the natural impulse must be broken in order to maintain the delusion in which the adult primate is trapped.

I became aware of this phenomenon in my mid-twenties. When my daughter said her first NO. Luckily for me, I was already proficient at the care and nurturing of my inner child. So, I replied with, "What a great word, would you be so kind and say it again?" I celebrated her "Power of NO" from the initial utterance. I understood that she was simply growing rather than being sinful or rebellious. I decided not to repeat the trauma I experienced as a child. It is a tragedy and a crime that parents are not more aware of the weight their actions place on their children and the repercussions they have on our world.

The insidious unseen self, rubs more salt in the wound by making us believe that our problems stem from invisible bullies "out there" rather than the physical caretakers who act as enforcers on their behalf. The real perceived bullies are our feelings inside, the ones crying out for our insightful inquiry and loving attention in the painful experiences of our lives.

The breaking of the *will* is a primary job of the invisible self, which is hired to divide and conquer the human biology. It is the job of religion to catch the confused human primate, as it gets older, and reinforce the deception through the collective dualistic belief of its social order. If a person has enough courage they might venture into more occult studies in which the "will" and its development are primary goals. This venture is the attempted recovery of the *lost will of the child* through the conceptualized "holy guardian angel" or "higher self." The imagination, having been suppressed and ridiculed, conjures up grandiose imagery to return to its forgotten land. Dream imagery is a perfect example of how our "organic dream machine" processes the crushing pains of innocence.

In addition to the breaking of the *will*, the abuse of the imagination is just as damaging. Here, the *originations* of the young primate are stepped on and humiliated in a myriad of ways. Nightmares are dismissed by telling the child to "stop being a cry baby" and the toddler is forced back to sleep in a lonely room not to interrupt the parent's proclivities. It is the dream made sarcastically insignificant, the imaginary friend belittled, or the scary drawing crumpled up and tossed into the trash. The young person learns to doubt their native impulses when they could be developing them under the watchful eyes of their wise caregivers. The amnesia from which our species suffers (forgetting their primate origins) causes an alien-like insensitivity toward children and others. Because humans are disassociated from their mammalian self through the story of religion, their instinctive sensibilities are suppressed.

In our culture we are encouraged to dream and create and pursue entrepreneurial ventures. We are inspired by the power of an idea and its potential when cultivated by commitment and focus. What you will hear less about is the power of a dark thought spawned from the shame in a child's life or about the slow and subtle growth of this tiny seed of self-doubt and *the effect it will have on our world*. It is here, in the young fertile organism, that the leaves of nightmares are grown—where the roots of self-hatred secure their dark future.

It is my belief that when a child has been robbed of their visionary rights that they gravitate toward religion and spirituality to regain their *Subjective autonomy*. The imaginary friend, who was taken away prematurely, is replaced by a socially acceptable, invisible buddy in the sky, such as Jesus. The popular religious icons serve to validate a native need; the need to grow, through our imagination, into capable adults. In this light, it is easy to see why mature, educated people find solace in the fantastical fairy tales of the esoteric. The passion of the preacher is really the voice of the child claiming their Subjective rights through the orthodox bullhorn.

A suppressed and ridiculed imagination can lead to delusion. Our world is filled with adults who believe in religious and spiritual stories that defy rational thought. In fact, policymakers who adhere to the biblical tale are considered more respectable in the eyes of their peers and the audience they entertain. We have here a shocking display of cognitive dissonance. On one hand, there is the desire for ethical policy and on the other hand the policy makers believe in a bible that is filled with violence against humans—a book which contradicts the facts of science. They want to make the world a better place, yet, they believe god is going to destroy the earth and save the elect—you cannot be operating on all cylinders and believe this contradiction. It is a story of shame, fear, judgment, abuse and slavery.

The crazy thing about imagination is that it has required thousands of years to develop in humans. The ability to think and create stems from the innumerable mutations that have occurred during the process of natural selection. Our brains did not develop overnight due to some superior being magically causing us to appear in the twinkle of an eye. It is an absurd proposition considering the overwhelming evidence for evolution. Growing humans is a slow and diverse process that has taken approximately 200 thousand years to accomplish, preceded by 4 billion years to reach the mammalian stage.

Religion and spirituality have suppressed the understanding of evolution since its discovery by Darwin. A true understanding of human origins would not only remove the nagging "who am I" question, but provide good reasons to honor a child's inner world. The "ghost in the machine" model would be understood as a product of biology and humans would awaken to themselves as a species. There would be no *theocrapic* (disgust for theistic babble) ideology passed on. In my opinion, if you split a child into a body and a soul, you plant the seeds for an unpredictable, socially acceptable, schizophrenic adult. In other words, you deform a life.

Chapter 6

EMOTION

"From Death comes life, from sacrifice, bliss."

"Do not withdraw from the world when you realize how horrible it is but realize that this horror is simply the foreground to a wonder. Participate in it."
— Joseph Campbell

"The oldest and strongest emotion of mankind is fear, and the oldest and strongest kind of fear is fear of the unknown."
— H.P. Lovecraft

There is a bonding agent that holds the story together. It is the primary administrator of all pain and suffering in humans. It is responsible for the proliferation of religion, spiritual beliefs and political dogmas. This substance is so strong that its effect can cause the most ethical among us to commit unthinkable crimes. I'm talking about *emotion* in the strongest sense and *feeling* in the subtler.

Human feeling is the fuel that drives our actions in life. A person may feel anger one moment, indifference the next and peace in another. The healthiest among us view negative feelings as a natural occurrence while others treat these with fervent disdain. However one slices and dices the impassioned buffet we are sentimental creatures. While the narcissist polishes her protective cold mask the criminal sits in a lonely cell regretting the emotional outburst that led to the crime. As the mother weeps at home for her imprisoned child the addict recovers their natural feeling and returns to sanity.

Feelings ignite the spiritual story from forbidden fantasies to elaborate musings, emotions are expressed in a myriad of ways. In the religious story dark emotions spark imaginings of the devil, demons and invisible predatory forces while in the modern spiritual story our feelings ignite conspiracy, karma, negative energies and low vibrations—even alien meddling is on the table as a scapegoat for these primal affections. The hunt and prey in our DNA lurk behind the curtain of our Subjective entertainment.

In the religious community life is filled with emotion from the conversion of faith to the baptism in water. Life for the chosen is fueled by affection, communion and adoration for the image of the divine. The Sunday service ranges from wild outbursts of theistic exaltation to laying prostrate before a bloody deity or risen savior. For many, it is a peaceful, sentimental and nostalgic moment in their week.

Feelings function in real-time, they are constant from birth until death. To feel is to be alive. The heart beats, the lungs breathe, yet no one controls these functions—they just happen. Conflict arises when the flow of emotion becomes frozen in time due to traumatic events along life's path. These are moments when a person's life takes an abrupt halt; when they are led to believe something that runs contrary to their intuitions. What was once, a natural movement of feelings, solidifies into a dam holding back the waters of life.

Expressing emotion is primary to being human. Experiencing positive and negative feelings and every nuance in between. It is what the human experience is all about—whether you're conducting an ethical life or a criminal life, emotions drive us.

Children do not easily assimilate the painful events in their lives. Even with the help of an understanding adult, the process of healing can take a long time. The confusion of unfinished business mixed with closeted emotions creates a cocktail of inner conflict. Feelings, once cherished, become distant memories for the individual seeking refuge in their effort to escape reality. Overwhelmed by the re-stimulation of negative life experiences, irrational psychological patterns emerge further alienating the child abuse survivor from their natural sense of wellbeing. It is a vicious pattern that culminates in a religious conversion, a mid-life crisis, drugs, suicide or an awakening.

I believe emotional suppression fueled by a shamed imagination lies at the root of society's ailments. It is the *believing* leaders of religion that keep the "denial circus" going decade after decade. We have, for too long, supported this tyranny of delusion. We have given the guru and the preacher the stage one too many times. It is time to wake up and replace the preacher with the human teacher—a human who *is* the intelligence of their whole organism.

Religion fills the gap for the person who is disconnected from, or traumatized by, close communal ties. Long forgotten feelings from the days of our innocence, before the deluge of our forgetfulness, find a new home in this "controlled collective environment." The convert becomes a believer *because* of the emotions that lie underneath the threshold of their awareness.

These native emotions are so intense that they can easily be misunderstood. The appeal to assign religious and spiritual ideology is just too tempting especially in the company of the family-like congregation showering their "sleeping potion" of love on the newly surrendered adult infant.

Irrational stories of talking snakes and people rising from the dead are blended with the warm embrace of the faithful. "Father and Mother God" replace the faulty or missing parents of childhood. Trust is regained and attachment is secured by the emotional glue therein.

When people attribute their personal pain to the spiritual story I think they are avoiding the reality of their lives. I discovered from my individual work, in lieu of my spiritual beliefs at the time, that true healing occurred in the context of my life—the one I was living here and now. Whenever I considered a past life, an evil force, or some ambiguous energy to be the cause of my problem, there were only temporary bouts of relief. I knew from experience that the nightmares and dreams in my life were direct reflections of a trauma in the past, a present issue, or a future fear. It was accurate, I could see the pattern and it helped me understand my healing process.

I believe that when a person opens up to the possibility that evolution is true, a shift takes place in their consciousness. The importance of awakening to our evolutionary origins is paramount because irrational ideas about "who we are" fuel our sense of separateness. If you assign your emotions to Subjective fantasies, then you are living in a dream state and your natural biological impulses will be misinterpreted.

Evolution explains our emotions with surprising clarity. Take a look at the environment from which we have grown, planet earth, the wind, water, earth, plant and animal life—all reflect our biology. With all of its natural beauty and violence, our species experienced a kaleidoscope of feelings from intense "horror," (being eaten alive) to undisturbed epochs of peace. Spiritual stories that differ from culture to culture and person to person describe events that are fueled by the emotions and perceptions of the time.

It is not the focus of this writing to teach the science of evolution, but to paint a picture of the tremendous difference between the spiritual story and the facts of our evolutionary origins.

I encourage you to learn more about evolution through comparative physiology and biochemistry, corresponding anatomy, paleontology, observed natural selection, observed speciation, evidence from artificial selection, computation and mathematical iteration. There are numerous subjects, from DNA and genetics to fossil records and embryonic development, to explore. I think that after a cursory overview, you will wonder why the majority of our species are still walking around in the dark ages of metaphysics. For this is the story of our species, based on hard evidence—not superstition or imaginary whims.

Chapter 7

IDENTIFICATION

"Everything which shocks you, disrupts you, disturbs you can be your friend. Everything which allows you to sleep, to be complacent, hinders you."
— Christopher Hyatt

"The world is indeed comic, but the joke is on mankind."
— H. P. Lovecraft

When we identify with something we associate our "self" with "something else" such as our parents, peers, teachers or cultural icons. This type of identification can be useful in developing a rational reflection within ourselves. We draw from the best character traits in others to heighten our survival rate and increase our happiness throughout life. In the best case scenario, we have a solid sense of autonomy and a clear boundary between our own thoughts and intuitions and those we adopt. Self-determination is never replaced by an external force and we are attuned to the rhythm of our biology.

The process of identification goes terribly wrong when a child replaces their self-will with the determination of another. It is resigned under force either by neglected needs or volatile abuse. *Abandonment* can lead a child to generate a "needy self" that will demand attention from its caregivers, where *forceful abuse* can elicit a rebellious and bitter identity. Because the false self is "constructed" in reaction to the opposing parental force, it must be fed, emotionally, to stay alive. This is accomplished by acting out the dictates of the false self in order to validate the child's original premise, which was to "solve a problem." Because the child is not innately wrong they must "be right" in their origination which is achieved through a tailor made false self and its fervent actions of punishment to set the record straight. This Subjective turmoil continues throughout life until new social experiences contradict the invested identity.

When someone is trapped in an identity, parts of their original self are blended with the reactive content of their false self. Attempting to distinguish between them is like trying to find a needle in a haystack. The reason for this difficulty is because the mind functions like a mirror. When a child is born, it peers into the eyes of the parents in gleeful admiration due to the symbiotic relationship that feeds its needs. There is no self, but the feeling of being taken care of. If the parents are nurturing the young person grows into their natural personality which could be described as a native *felt-sense* of self. Their self-determinism is untainted which allows for an individualized expression.

If the child is born to parents suffering from self-hatred, narcissism, religious indoctrination or unhealed psychological trauma, then these toxic elements are reflected and assumed as "self" by the child. This infection can also occur in families where random harmful events invade the "safe zone" of the child from a trusted outsider. When the act of identification occurs, innate elements of the child's personality are swallowed up by the feeling of overwhelm.

For instance, let's say that a parent reprimands a child for saying "no," and when the child displays anger for this suppressive act against its will, the parent responds with a spanking. Over time, the child's innate and "justified" anger is crushed by the reinforcing commands of the dominant adult. The implied order, "do not get angry or assert your will," along with the imprinted physical punishment make it almost impossible to recover authentic anger from reactive.

Thus, the person growing up becomes very confused about their feelings and the boundaries that protect them. Anger is natural, but the command to "not be angry" creates internal conflict.

A person might adopt many identities, in their efforts to survive throughout life, which all culminate into a master "broken self." All these selves are part of the same club—dualism. Their commonality lies in being phantoms of the biology. They all need to feed on external attention or rejection to generate enough emotion to keep them alive. They are given permission to exist solely by the "decision" of their creator (the human primate) who has forgotten its own powers. Human beings have a powerful imagination with the ability to create something and then forget they created it—this is the plight of identification.

I remember the moment I witnessed my own false self. I saw the "self" I was identified with as a broken person who was a slave to the past. I was justifying my life based on an image of the collective memories of trauma and abuse. I realized that thoughts were "lit up" by the vision itself. Like a projector and a screen, I saw my thoughts as images brought to light by the act of looking at them. The self-construct I was looking at was merely a hologram of pain that existed locally in my body. It had no more basis in reality than did an image of a hamburger I had for lunch. But because I had invested so much energy into it, a familiarity grew that made the Subjective "image" of myself indistinguishable from the actual living, breathing, "me" of the present moment.

It took some time to integrate this realization into my life experience, but the chronic attachment had been interrupted. I realized my existence was in the present moment. The dream of the past was over, and I was simply myself—a deeply feeling, intelligent human organism. Over time, I learned a process called "Focusing" [1] that gave me the tools to take this process even deeper. I learned how to develop a relationship with myself at a core inner level (In the last chapter of this book I introduce the Focusing Method).

Our society is filled with people unknowingly suffering from some form of toxic identification. From erroneous religious beliefs to narcissistic behavior, the split in personality feeds a sense of separation from the natural world. Because this split occurs typically in childhood, the ground is set for the ultimate flowering of religious and spiritual identification.

There are many reasons why humans adhere to religious and metaphysical belief systems. Common among them are: comfort and assurance, fear of the unknown, tradition, lack of responsibility, guilt, desperation, the search for answers, and socialization. But it is childhood indoctrination that lies at the root of religious adherence. *I believe religious indoctrination is child abuse.* Parents who teach their children dualistic belief systems based on the supernatural arrest their child's direct perception of the natural environment. The invisible story is insinuated by the local parental gods and the child's imagination is prematurely replaced with externally enforced fantasies.

The issuing overlord's decrees are never questioned unless the child finds good reason to rebel. This may require many decades of filtering before they retrieve their authentic voice. Where it gets tricky is the maturing person might find their rebellious identity so delicious and rewarding that they may never break free of the chains that are attached to the object of rebellion—the dominant caregivers. If one can "own" the story by understanding the construct from which it is made and retrieve the lost parts that were trapped in the false identity, then, the rebel identity can be adopted as a preference rather than a crutch.

I suppose the spiritual trance is harder to break than the religious one because the delusion is more difficult to distinguish. You have a quasi-cloud of ideas that include wonderful concepts of openness and altruism without the blatant anthropomorphism of religion. Love, hope and peace become new spiritual identities rather than natural expressions of the human experience.

When people identify with noble concepts there is an impulse to parade them along with a tendency to diminish the effort required to earn them. This parading of Gandhi-like godliness fails when tested under the fire of friendship and social interaction. I have noticed this in people who say one thing and do another. They might espouse world peace but do nothing about it. They might preach to you the virtues of love in such an invasive way that your inner peace feels threatened by the desperate performance.

Love is not a word, it is an action that comes from a biological feeling and accrued awareness; one that required millions of years to be felt and expressed in the human primate. There would be no reason to wear peace and love like jewelry if these attributes were embodied. These virtues are a natural result of life experiences, they are developed, not assigned, they are *the pearls without price*. However, in the religious and spiritual arena they are put on display (in many cases) to elicit attention. Where there is a self-concept, enemies are needed to fuel the conflict, or, as in this scenario—friends to polish the mirror.

One of the most effective tactics of the invisible self is to brand "thinking" or as I call it "radical curiosity" as counter-productive. Just like religion, spirituality positions the mind as the enemy and the heart as savior. I thought I was liberated from this when I left Christianity until I ventured into spirituality and was told to get out of my "thinking mind." This unwelcome advice would come to me in many forms over the years such as "get into your heart" or "get out of your head" as if the organism was suffering from biological dualism. The heart doesn't say to the head, "hey, can you keep it down I'm trying to feel down here." The human body does not cut itself up into sections as the spiritualists are led to believe based on modern and ancient holy writ.

I do not see the value of separating humans into a body, soul and spirit. We don't do this with any other mammals, so why do we do it with ourselves? Thinking and fresh ideas arise naturally from the rhythm of one's internal felt-sense. It is the process artists demonstrate to humanity—to express our individuality in real-time, as a living process, rather than a "copied" idea.

The answer lies in misunderstanding our internal processes and by identifying with the mind and its forms. It appears that the challenge for primates, to recoup their natural intelligence, is to hack through their Subjective jungle and make it to the other side sanely. Childhood fantasies must be worked out so that they become cognitive adults who can make rational decisions.

Our inner world can be our paint brush or our bullwhip depending on our depth of identification.

Identification spawns a myriad of problems for human beings like subverting the body as a slave for ideologies. The natural is denied and belief empowered until confronted by an overwhelming opposing force. This usually comes in the form of a tragic accident, the death of a loved one, broken relationships or reaching rock bottom. Not until our emotional investment is jolted out of position can we begin to grow anew in the broken soil of our imagination.

I will end this chapter with a quote by Christopher Hyatt in his book "Undoing Yourself,"[2] which helped break up the *fallow ground* of my own thinking and eventually shatter the mirror of identification.

> *You must stop finding yourself in misery,*
> *in cranial pride—historic stupidity.*
> *You must stop strutting around like a fattened COW.*
> *You must stop bowing down to your mistakes.*
> *You must stop idol worshiping.*
> *You must surrender your misery.*
> *You must stop acting surprised . . .*
> *when something happens to you.*
> *For it is the same old thing.*
> *You must stop reacting to things as you always HAVE.*
> *You must stop proving your story.*
> *You must stop extending the past into the present and future.*
> *You must stop defending your stupidity YOUR SLEEP.*
> *You must stop defending YOUR MISERY.*
> *YOU MUST WAKE UP.*
> *(Emphasis in original text)*

Chapter 8

CHILDHOOD TRAUMA

> *"Dissociation (being split-off from one's deepest truth) mimics enlightenment – but it isn't enlightenment. People who are dissociated live in great peace. But this is only because they have blocked their negative feelings. The enlightened person resolves his negatives feelings, and thus his peace is not false."*
> — Daniel Mackler

> *"Memories and possibilities are even more hideous than realities."*
> — H.P. Lovecraft

If there is one factor I could assign to the problems of our world, it would be childhood trauma. Trauma forces children into their Subjective world where primal instincts transform into looming darkness. The "dweller on the threshold" is the term used by the metaphysical tradition for this penetrating fear. The uncertain eyes of self-hatred are the result of suppressed natural impulses that lurk behind both the positive and negative self-image. However real these phantoms appear to be, they are merely the Subjective ghosts of the past crying out for our love. Biological expressions of pain, long forgotten, in the whirlwinds of our lives.

The person who is frozen inside the memories of loss and abandonment is haunted by a profound and abiding sadness. The feelings of unfinished business plague their existence like a scary movie running non-stop in the background. There is no rest for the person trapped in the mirror of their false self. The nagging feeling of "not-real" won't go away. It is as if their very core is screaming for freedom and gasping for air while slipping below the surface of cognition. Yet, the terror that awaits them in the bottomless pit of the unconscious is the admission of their participation in the lie—*that all identities were created and sustained by their own imaginings.* Owning up to this plan begins with an admission of cunning human genius, something which is unpopular in a culture that assigns responsibility to invisible authority rather than the creative primate.

Because the false self is not real there is more at stake. The feeling of "no-self" is tantamount to physical death in the psyche of the adult because the biological investment (into the image) comes crashing down once the illusion is *seen*. This "loss" is anticipated on deeper levels and avoided because being "found out" is not in the interest of the blind primate operative. Just like the person who complains about their hand being stuck in a jar because they won't let go of the desired object, resolution only occurs when the object is released or the glass shatters. Humans do not like the feeling of "being wrong" because of the vast lengths of time they "had" to be right to survive, so confronting a false Subjective self can be daunting.

The person suffering from childhood trauma does not believe in the evidence that lies before them. They could stumble upon a relationship with a person who is genuine and kind, and who offers to love and support them, but the emotionally charged, repugnant, invisible self, (that the person believes themselves to be) will not allow reality to challenge its certainties. There is much invested here. This splitting off in the formative years carries a sacred, righteous indignation at the perceived threat to its imagined realities.

The temptation of the human (whose false self becomes threatened through life experiences) is to adopt a new fantasy into which their delusion can persist, and religion and metaphysics become the new territory for expression. The hungry wayward spirit gravitates to a believer, guru, pastor, or group (people who live and organize their lives around the invisible self and its story) which rekindles the *feeling* of home. Supernatural stories provide fantastical environments that include the social interaction and parental approval the inner child craves. Unfortunately, they are unreal and distract the individual from accessing the source of the trauma which is found in the life they are living.

If a person is fortunate enough to develop an adult self who takes charge of their inner child, then tricking the invisible self at its own game becomes possible. This is a step in the right direction because the identification with the negative self is not challenged, but validated, by the appearance of the inner adult who agrees never to leave them. I believe this is a healthy act, a stepping stone. Healing is now originating from the very biology that created the delusion in the first place. The identities in the mind that were compartmentalized can have a context from which to bridge themselves, and the rejected inner child is no longer trapped alone in the phantasmagorical haunting of their Subjective world. Rather than using grandiose spiritual stories to distract oneself from their actual life, the Subjective is used in the context of the natural world (parenting) and the real issues are accessed and confronted.

The power of a child's perception and imagination should never again be underestimated by adults, if for no other reason, then the survival of our species. The simple act of a father rejecting or shaming his daughter's behavior might feel like normal behavior to him, but to her, it feels like a stake has been driven into her heart forever. His callous response may seem harmless (being alienated from his own sensitivities), but, to the child, her world has collapsed. As this insensitive behavior toward the child continues, it only serves to enforce the emotionally fueled delusion of the un-healed adult.

There are many occasions when life presents a person with a choice to either confront their disillusion self or enforce it. The payoff with drug abuse is that it relieves the discomfort of the psychotic split and forces the attention to the biology. The physical pain of withdrawal serves to "overwhelm" the attachment to the delusional self and bring the person to the act of surrender. Because our culture assigns our "ground of being" to invisible realms, the "higher self" idea becomes the object to surrender to—and yet, it is just another concept to overcome. The "feeling" of the higher self is the key in this experience, but the un-awakened primate who is still trapped in the Subjective mirror is unaware that this fantasy is actually their biology scratching across the chalk board of their ego to get their attention.

Just like the inner parent, the higher self provides another bridge for the helpless feelings of the terrified secret child. Both lower and higher self-concepts reflect the range of the evolutionary development of the brain, ranging from the primal structures "hindbrain" to the cognitive master controller—the cerebrum.

The mid-life crisis is another milestone in the hope for freedom from identification. The unchallenged self-concept of human life reaches a breaking point where reality and illusion come clashing together. If the person survives, they will begin to see their life as a dream from which they are awakening. For others, it will feel as if their whole life has been one big lie. They come to the startling realization that they have been adrift upon a sea of assumptions. What is occurring here is the breakdown of the invisible self. The conceptual "I" is falling apart and the *felt-sense* of the organism is coming through. It is *that* which creates the concept (biology) rather than the concept itself that is awakening from the trance.

The word "human" in itself is a concept and what it points to is an existence that is occurring spontaneously in real-time. It is this realization that cuts through the egoistic fog that keeps humans wandering and reaching outward for resolution. True healing comes in the form of self-care. This involves nutrition, education, healthy peers and turning inward toward an authentic way of life. Traits such as honesty, commitment, reason, caring and integrity are the hallmarks of authenticity. Recovering adults need an environment where the real world is accepted—not pretended away—as in the case of the religious arena.

Authentic healing comes from accepting reality "as it is" rather than how we wish it to be or how we were told it is. It is better to accept the mystery and honestly admit "I don't know" rather than to surrender to unseen powers that mimic the natural world. This consigning of "will" to the God or mental image reflects the memories of parental abuse still vivid in the child's biology. Feelings of abandonment in the heart of the innocent ignite primitive emotions that express themselves in grandiose inner landscapes—*The whole world is falling apart.*

Spirituality gives the delusional self a fantasy world to live in. It is a playground for the inner child to retrieve its imagination. It can be useful only as a stepping stone because its attractiveness allures the hungry child like a moth to a flame. Spirituality, with its invisible self and dimensional realms, functions like a flashlight in the eyes of humanity, blinding their way. When this occurs, identification solidifies once again, and spirituality, just like a beautiful carnivorous plant, traps its prey.

The "need to be seen" is the saga of the conceptual inner child. The identity created in religious and spiritual systems becomes the Frankenstein of the wounded. The child expresses its deficiencies through the toxic phantom in proportion to the depth of the unconscious pain. It is an expansive invisible self in an unbounded adventure land where anything one thinks instantly comes true—immediate manifestation. The pain of the unthinkable acts of the past, which were perpetrated on the young heart, are now linked with the physical world as "painful," while the Subjective becomes the *safe zone*. This is the beginning of psychotic behavior.

> *Once the wounded child awakens to its human self, a primal scream emerges from the depths of denial like the Kraken released from its underwater prison.*

The infant requires nothing but love, caring and integration into the world into which it was born. However, when the natural is rejected, shamed, denied, invalidated or abandoned, the child is forced to succumb to a lie. This denial becomes the kindling from which their primal scream will one day ignite the flame that burns in the quest for freedom and justice. Unfortunately, the fight for one's true voice is crippled by the emotionally handicapped braveheart. The sword in the heart must be integrated to see the battlefield with unobstructed eyes.

The invisible self is so cunning that kind words become food for its insatiable appetite. The identified primate takes offense at any disagreement with its perceived reality and finds refuge in the fuzzy world of spirituality where belief is unchallenged and thinking discouraged. The bright, beautiful, spiritual self, with its non-physical evolution, blinds the wounded seeker while fueling the twisted psychology of the crying heart. Dissecting the egoistic construct requires semantic surgery and a radical acceptance for the felt-sense inside.

It is in our denial of the natural that the infection of insanity continues. Our children need to be born into the world *"as it is"* and treated in proportion to their biological dictates. The insensitivity toward the children of our species and the profound effect it has on our world has yet to be understood by the majority of Homo sapiens. If there is one scripture I would quote, in light of this tragic dilemma, which screams out within the cell bars of orthodoxy, it is this;

> *But whoso shall offend one of these little ones which believe in me, it were better for him that a millstone were hanged about his neck, and that he were drowned in the depth of the sea.*
> — Matthew 18:6

Of course, the "believe in me" part is another example of how the invisible self, hijacks natural truth. If one were to paraphrase this verse I don't think they could say it in a way that wasn't offensive. Allow me to try:

> *Stop harming children or die!*

It appears that the writer of this verse was serious about the consequences of child neglect and abuse. When one looks at humankind as a species, this brief statement makes a lot of sense.

Purely, by right of natural birth, children qualify for respect in all of their biological expression. Imagination, feelings, sensitivities, perceptions and proclivities are the working tools of the developing human *being*. Just because children are smaller in size than towering adults, the tender, physical organism is none the less worthy of human rights. The abolishment of physical and psychological abuse should be encouraged by our civilization as a means of survival for our species. Both nature and nurture must be taken seriously. Socially accepted fantastical ideologies must be confronted and evolution *realized* for the understanding of our natural existence to arise within our collective consciousness.

Self-indulgent fantasies, paraded in the mortuaries we call churches and temples, have had their day in the sun. The platform of the metaphysical teacher, who has basked in narcissistic glory for eons, must now be replaced by people who live in their full human expression. I look forward to the day when the statement, "you are going to hell" is brought up to par with a psychological death threat and seen as the bullying it really is.

The cultural allowance given to the televangelist to preach cosmic threats on our television sets reflects the insensitivity we have toward the inner world of our species. The same goes for the guru who insinuates universal repercussions for bad thoughts. I think planting the seed "you are a spirit" in a child's mind should be considered child abuse and not an option for an evolved civilization—they are our future!

Planet of Lost Primates

If an alien visitor were to come to this planet, what do you think their opinion would be of our species? What would be the assessment? What would be the introduction speech to mankind? May I take the liberty of speculating? Here goes:

Hello Earthlings. We have just arrived on your planet and already we have discovered a big problem. Because we come from the outer reaches of space we can tell you that there are no invisible versions of your species flying around up there. We hate to break the news to you, but your race is not that evolved. We know you are making up for something. We know that you just don't like being the primates that you are, so you concoct grandiose stories of yourselves. Trust us, we have been around the universe for a long time and you people are suffering from an identity crisis. *There is nothing wrong with being human.* Give it a shot, you may be able to interact with off planet civilizations before you know it. In the meantime, stop pretending and stop denying your inner pain, it is there to guide you . . . listen to it.

Part 3 | I Am Human

Chapter 9

THE HUMAN ANIMAL

"I think the discomfort that some people feel in going to the monkey cages at the zoo is a warning sign."
— Carl Sagan

"Oh, shame on you, you animal."
— Unknown

I find it interesting that the root word for spirit is the equivalent for animal. The word "animal" comes from the Latin word *animalis*, meaning "having breath." However, in stark contrast to the spiritual self, which is a Subjective experience, the evidence for the human animal is overwhelming. Let's look at the definition for animal:

According to Merriam-Webster:

> Any kingdom (Animalia) of living things, including many-celled organisms as well as the single-celled ones (as protozoans) that typically differ from plants in having cells without cellulose walls, in lacking chlorophyll and the capacity for photosynthesis, in requiring more complex food materials (as proteins), in being organized to a greater degree of complexity, and in having the capacity for spontaneous movement and rapid motor responses to stimulation.

Humans share genes with all living organisms thanks to millions of years of evolution. The percentage of genes that organisms share reveals their similarities and intimacy in the evolutionary tree of life. Let's take a look at the evidence for the human animal from "What Does It Mean to Be Human?" by authors Richard Potts and Christopher Sloan.[1]

Evidence for the Human Animal:

- Modern humans – 99.9% genetically similar
- You and bananas – 60% similar
- You and chickens – 75% similar
- You and mice – 85% similar
- You and chimpanzees – 98.8% similar
- You and gorillas – 98.4% similar
- You and orangutans – 96.9% similar
- You and rhesus monkeys – 93% similar

Now, let's take a look at the evidence for the spiritual being:

- Spiritual Being – 0%
- Biological Subjective Environment – 100%

Description of the human primate: Human primates are characterized by having a large brain relative to body size; they are capable of language, introspection, abstract reasoning, and problem solving. They have a far greater knack for tools than any other species on Earth and are the only species known to build fires, cook their food and clothe themselves. Humans have a talent for using systems of symbolic communication such as language for self-expression, the exchange of ideas and organization. They understand and influence their environment, by manipulating phenomena through science, philosophy, mythology and religion.

Description of a Spiritual being: Spiritual beings are characterized by invisibility. Because they are invisible we can only assume they exist, so, let's work from a hypothesis. Spiritual beings exist somewhere in the head or heart of a human primate and appear to *use* the body for learning experiences on Terra Firma. Their existence is communicated from human to human usually with an impressive story about their ability to defy the natural laws of existence. They love to utilize groups to promote their message which may come in the form of a myth, creation story or a future scenario that involves the destruction of the material world. It is suspected, by some, that spiritual beings are extremely jealous of the natural world because they are nothing more than a figment of the imagination. This might explain their compulsive and obsessive behavior in trying to convince others they are real, and that the natural world is an illusion. The end of the world scenarios they conjure up reveal their Napoleon whit and superiority complex.

To bring the matter home, let's take a short trot into human evolution and see how that compares to the story of "spiritual" origins.

> The evolution of our species originated in Africa approximately 200,000 years ago. Our lineage branched off from a species of chimpanzee some 5 million years ago. The first of our species to move out of Africa was Homo erectus, and together with Homo Heidelbergensis, are considered to be the immediate ancestors of modern humans. Approximately, 125,000-60,000 years ago we populated Eurasia; 40,000 years ago, Australia; and 15,000 years ago, America. Hawaii, New Zealand and Madagascar were

> populated between the years AD 300 and 1280.
>
> About 12,000 years ago, agriculture developed into a common practice, along with the domestication of plants and animals, which spurred on the growth of civilization. Humans established various forms of government, Religion, and culture around the world, unifying people within a region which led to the development of states and Empires. The rapid advancement of scientific and medical understanding in the 19th and 20th centuries led to the development of fuel-driven technologies and improved health, causing the human population to rise exponentially. With individuals widespread in every continent except Antarctica, humans are a cosmopolitan species, and by 2012, their population was estimated to be around 7 billion.[2]

When searching for concise answers to the origin of spirit, one immediately comes face to face with the allusiveness and ambiguity of the topic. Definitions depend on the physical location of the culture, its animals and landscape. The explanation for the invisible ranges from a non-quantifiable substance, and a pre-existing eternal soul, to animal Spirits, ghosts and demons.

Evidence for the *spiritual identity* can be discovered in the human Subjective experience and evidence for the *human animal* can easily be found by anyone willing to study evolution. There requires no journey to India, no need to fast or pray, no commitment to meditation and certainly no need to attend church services. All that is required is an open mind and the ability to comprehend the evidence gathered from the thousands of years of research our species has gathered. Let's take a look at the human genome.

> The closest living relatives of humans are chimpanzees (genus Pan) and gorillas (genus Gorilla). With the sequencing of both the human and chimpanzee genome, current estimates of similarity between human and chimpanzee DNA sequences range between 95% and 99%. By using the technique called a molecular clock, which estimates the time required for the number of divergent mutations to accumulate between two lineages, the approximate date for the split between lineages can be calculated. The gibbons (Hylobatidae) and orangutans (genus Pongo) were the first groups to split from the line leading to humans, then gorillas, followed by the chimpanzees and bonobos. The splitting date between human and chimpanzee lineages is placed around 4-8 million years ago, during the late Miocene epoch.[2]

It appears that to maintain the belief in a spiritual self, one has to suspend rational thought and trade facts for faith. The answers to the big questions "who am I?" and "where did I come from?" have been answered. However, in the mind of the believer, the addiction to the invisible feeds the monster of delusion in a never-ending loop of seeking the unattainable.

The spiritual world need not be discarded and replaced only with the knowledge of the human animal. Rather, the window into the vast inner world of humanity can be cleansed of its archaic tint. It is time to celebrate mankind's Subjective universe with new eyes and develop a deeper relationship to the fresh, ongoing impulses and energies of the living, breathing human being. A being capable of radically changing its experience *in* the world—from the inside out—as well as change the experience *of* the world for its species.

Chapter 10

UNFATHOMABLE EVOLUTION

"We are the local embodiment of a Cosmos grown to self-awareness. We have begun to contemplate our origins: star-stuff pondering the stars; organized assemblages of ten billion, billion, billion atoms considering the evolution of atoms; tracing the long journey by which, here at last, consciousness arose. Our loyalties are to the species and the planet. We speak for Earth. Our obligation to survive is owed not just to ourselves, but also to that Cosmos, ancient and vast, from which we spring."
— Carl Sagan

"There are not many persons who know what wonders are opened to them in the stories and visions of their youth; for when as children we learn and dream, we think but half-formed thoughts, and when as men we try to remember, we are dulled and prosaic with the poison of life. But some of us awake in the night with strange phantasms of enchanted hills and gardens, of fountains that sing in the sun, of golden cliffs overhanging murmuring seas, of plains that stretch down to sleeping cities of bronze and stone, and of shadowy companies of heroes that ride caparisoned white horses along the edges of thick forests; and then we know that we have looked back through the ivory gates into that world of wonder which was ours before we were wise and unhappy."
— H.P. Lovecraft

Most humans are unaware of the unfathomable evolutionary record. It is this lack of understanding that creates so much confusion. Reduce the evolutionary time line down to the Bible's 6000-year creation story and it serves only to validate a false impression. Consider for a moment the 4.5-billion-year history of life on earth where man did not show up until just a few seconds ago on this time-line. When history is put into perspective from an evolutionary standpoint, time takes on a whole new meaning and dwarfs the childish stories of our inherited spiritual beliefs.

We have been locked into a prison of time based solely on the dates of our imagined Gods. Behind the veil of 2000 years lies a landscape of scattered relics and speculations. Our ancient history only hints at a span of time incomprehensible to the modern mind. Superstition and ignorance maintain the trance of our species even in the face of devastating counter proof.

We have been evolving, and the evidence for this Darwinian gift has only increased over time. The voluminous data is so vast that science today compares creationism to that of the flat earth theory. Science has been ridiculed and distorted over the centuries by the religious. Nevertheless, it has only served to transform mankind from a superstitious creature to a consciously aware species. From medical breakthroughs and technological discoveries to ecological advances and social psychology, science is responsible for the quantum leap in human progress, not superstition. When I say science, I mean the radical curiosity and labor of living, breathing, *thinking* and *feeling* human beings.

The nostalgic feeling a spiritualist gets when they think of the past is rooted in a misrepresentation of history. Because they are seeing reality through the lens of belief—evidence is secondary. The religious person, who follows the Bible as an accurate portrayal of history, might find it rather dreamy to imagine sitting there alongside Moses while he parted the Red Sea. For the spiritualist, the Theosophical model might spark fantasies of Avalon and the Nights of the Round Table. In times of need, a surprise hallucination from Merlin may suffice. Interestingly enough, remove the identification and *literal belief with the content of the subjective* and Merlin could be a useful tool.

After many years of esoteric study I found one central theme; that the material world was invalidated for its *verification* of reality. For those who inherited this disconnection through some form of association with the phantom flue, the obvious becomes the ambiguous. However, for the person who accepts their natural existence and does not suffer from a resistance to the material— evidence becomes a welcome criterion for determining their cosmological view.

Spirituality is the smoke screen of history. It has led untold billions to believe fallacious versions of our existence. Consider for a moment the unfathomable span of time of our true history in comparison to the tiny spiritual version that keeps us stuck on the questions "who am I?" and "where did I come from?" The overwhelming evidence of evolution answers the big questions, but the spiritual story functions like a never-ending treadmill for the mind—it keeps us guessing or assuming because it does not exist. Just like the seeker of enlightenment who discovers after decades of searching, that enlightenment is an illusion, so humanity will one day awaken to their common ancestry.

Our unfathomable evolutionary past paints a picture vastly more immense than any spiritual story could ever create because it is raw and real, violent, dirty and beautiful—and because of that—it's spectacular! Our limited version is so small that the best we can do is assign a god or force behind it so that it appears big and sacred; and maybe, just maybe—no one will question it. We are addicted to the confidence we feel because of the grandiose stories of the invisible self.

In this view, we are no longer surprised by little Suzie's nightmare or the monster in the closet. The impulse to play sports with others reflects the competition of hunt and prey in our species. The desire to defend our territory, whether physical or Subjective, now makes sense.

The deep darkness and ghostly projections that emanate from within echo the violent past and its horrors. The "ringing true" of the feared thing within you is now brought into focus, diminishing its power. Reason and understanding replace terror and helplessness. The spiritual story has played a key role in alienating us from the truth causing an uneasy feeling of internal distrust and silent animosity. The pristine landscapes and daunting empires of our legacy fill our imaginations with boundless fantasies and creative intelligence. Our *peripheral vision* and *animal sensitivity* that we so easily assign to the (external) invisible is all owed to the true source—human subjectivity and evolution.

As the blinders come off, fate, déjà vu and synchronicity become the order of the day—not credited to some discarnate Force—but to nature. The body is no longer a servant in the house of the sorcerer. Nature is no longer expendable, and children are our greatest asset rather than our unconscious punching bags.

It is the religious story that not only disrupts our true history, but brainwashes organic intelligence. We are the real inheritors—not the orators of the intangible. We are history, evident in our breath, our skin and blood—not the fairy-tales of the incorporeal. We do not have bodies—*we are bodies!* What could possibly be wrong with *that* form of consciousness? It is all energy anyways. The disrespect toward the physical has only served to treat the body as expendable, and thus, the delusional mind continues its conquest of the natural world.

Did we trap ourselves in the image of our minds because we no longer wanted to be apes? Did we develop a prejudice toward the physical in order to evolve to a higher state? Did the human organism learn it could increase its survival rate by manipulating other bodies through the spiritual story? Are the cultural statues, cathedrals and monuments, which are positioned in key public places, there to remind us of the image over nature? Are we nearing the end of this delusion because the elephant in the room "evolution" is becoming too big to ignore?

Evolution provides answers to the questions for which our species yearns. We have, for centuries, lived with the nagging unseen thorn in our minds. Immersed in the blinding light of cultural dualism, we have inherited the memes of our ancestors. It appears the conceptualizing of nature helped humanity transit from tooth and claw to civilized primates; the stories of the sun, planets, birth and death, have affected our genes like fodder for the brain. Maybe the myths gave us the mental software to evolve from cave dwellers to rocket engineers? What is certain is that superstitions no longer serve a species when they stand in the way of evidence—no matter what anyone believes. The world is not flat!

Religion and spirituality have monopolized the sensitivities of the native, turning a precious natural thing into a concrete prison of symbols. It is the ultimate delusion of the primate; the sculpture of its self-disdain. It is none other than the emotionally charged concept in the mind of the believer who resists the fresh offerings of each new moment. The spiritual idea is based on outdated wisdom—a wisdom turned into absurdity. Like a melon left out in the sun for too long, its usefulness is left for the garbage heap. What this author is attempting to do is throw it into the compost bin.

Chapter 11

NATURAL INTELLIGENCE

> *"If we look straight and deep into a chimpanzee's eyes, an intelligent self-assured personality looks back at us. If they are animals, what must we be?"*
> — Frans de Waal

> *"Just because it's natural doesn't mean you can be as stupid as you want with it."*
> — Susan Lynn Peterson

We humans are naturally intelligent creatures.

When I say "intelligent" I am pointing to the stuff we are all born with. Every human is born with a beating heart, vital blood, a vast emotional kaleidoscope of feelings and imagination. All of this has grown through many thousands of years. A millennium of gained experience included with every human child. This kind of intelligence is "built in" rather than taught in school. It is the type of innate intelligence that requires watering, with care and understanding, for it to grow into its unique flower in the world.

I believe the metaphor of a flower is a perfect symbol for natural intelligence. Our religious systems have taught us to "train up a child in the way he should go, and when he is old he will not depart from it." (Proverbs 22:6) I couldn't disagree more. How about, *"feed a child what it needs, so when it gets grows up, it will "be" its own unique unpredictably creative self."*

Emotionally stable and vibrant children take to education far friendlier than those who are suffering from neglect. It is essential to understand the human being as a whole ecosystem when thinking about intelligence (the whole mind is the entire body). A well-educated person, who is emotionally bankrupt, is like a flower with a broken stem. We are feeling beings and it is through those feelings that we relate to our environment. We experience the world through our feelings and thoughts, it is where we *come from*. No matter how much education a person gets, without a healthy Subjective life, there exists an imbalance with their natural intelligence.

Natural intelligence looks upon another human being as they are, based on observation and experience, rather than uninvestigated self-indulgent projections. Making assumptions is the easy way to get the feeling of certainty that we crave. Internal curiosity, on the other hand, protects us from becoming duped by our own Subjective delusions. For example, we can investigate the recurring experiences that plague our lives and discover the belief behind pattern.

There is an assumption that people tend to make when pondering evolution, and that is the idea that being a primate allows for unethical behavior and a "survival of the fittest" mentality. When confronted with concerns such as these my response is to point out the difference between intelligence and belief.

The faithful often blame the theory of evolution for genocide. In the case of Nazism and the Hutu slaughter in Rwanda they fail to understand the context in which these events occurred. Political ideology, mixed with eugenics, justified horrific acts against perceived sub races. Yet, in no way, does evolution, as it is now understood, provide grounds to abuse our fellow human beings. Like everything in history, theories evolve and through that process innumerable mistakes have been made. It is not the evidence of evolution that kills people, but the ideology and beliefs that are assigned to it. Unfortunately, for our species, evolution does not provide a smooth path for progress nor has it ever suggested bad things won't happen. What it does offer is the ability to learn from our mistakes and increase our natural intelligence, discovering more ways to improve our survival and enjoy the experience.

The events of our individual and cultural histories are meant to inform us about our present state of affairs. Parking one's philosophy in the negative events of the past only serves to narrow the creativity of the present. Arguments that attempt to pin atrocious acts on evolution are inaccurate and misleading. Evolution in the context of our current understanding of social behavior, human rights, and ethical reasoning provides a stable base of knowledge from which we can improve the conditions in our world.

I see no reason to regress into the dark ages of eugenics as a social movement. Our understanding of the world with all its diversity has emerged into a holistic view of humanity. Morality and ethics are no longer the property of the church or the spiritual, rather, altruism is seen as a natural outcome of our shared genetic pool. *Redefining god and spirituality is necessary for our survival.*

But what about the animalistic acts of humans? Are not animal instincts responsible for murder, rape, torture, kidnapping and theft? What is the source of evil in our world? Where do humans get their killer instincts?

To answer these questions, let's use dogs as an example. Dogs have the built-in survival mechanisms to eat, sleep and nurture their young. They also have the innate drive to protect their pack and territory; thus, they bark, growl, and threaten to attack. All of these characteristics appear normal and healthy to the owner who takes good care of the dog. If you take this dog and put it into an abusive environment, the same normal characteristics may turn into a very toxic expression where people are bitten, or the dog runs away. If we put humans in the same context, I think it is easy to assume the same general outcome. But let's take it further.

A baby is born from the womb of a crack addicted mother. The father suffers from alcoholism, beats the mother, and leaves after years of domestic violence. The child goes to a public school where ridicule and violence from classmates are a daily occurrence. The mother becomes a Christian and begins teaching the child that he or she was born in sin and must be saved from eternal torture in Hell. She says, "our Father in heaven needed a blood sacrifice to atone for our sins, the world is about to end any minute, we must be on our best behavior." When the child reaches the teen years, drugs and alcohol are introduced, which further confuses the already mixed emotions of childhood. Thoughts of suicide haunt the emerging adult, and life becomes a struggle. Add physical violence, sexual assault, and gang association to the mix and there is a strong potential for violent crime. Even if a child has a specific negative genetic trait science tells us that those genes can remain dormant and with the proper nurturing environment positive genes can be turned on.

Natural intelligence is the key to understanding. When we fear what we don't know we amplify the assumptions made against the unknown. The intelligent remedy is to educate oneself on the topic and raise awareness for future decisions. The way of faith assigns the thing feared to our irrational emotional conclusions which serves to enforce belief and shun "real-time" fresh inquiry. Problem solving is narrowed down to the confines of the belief system and limits the fresh ideas that come from free thinking. New ways to survive don't come from outdated information, but from innovative ideas spawned from an *unchained imagination.*

We must raise our awareness. As a global community, it is in our best interest as a species to look upon another as our brother or sister rather than with predatory eyes. We are all connected. We are a global species where information, commerce and resources are shared. Intelligence need not be rejected as something machine-like or inhuman but celebrated as the organic expression of evolutionary wisdom that it is. It has taken us a long time to get where we are, and it is time to take our rightful place by setting down the crutch of the gods. It is time for us to understand and trust who we are and use our intelligence to create an amazing civilization.

A Spiritual Conspiracy

The definition of a conspiracy typically involves the coordinated efforts of a few organized individuals, or groups that form and carry out a calculated plan. I am using the word as a metaphor for something that cannot be pinned down to one person or group. The conspiracy I am talking about is subtle, yet pervasive, invisible and global. Its tentacles reach deep into the very fabric of our society. Its blueprint uncovered in our psyches. Its plans projected onto the canvas of our vision. It cannot be seen by most, and its insidious nature feeds off the life of the human primate.

In searching for the answers to my plight, I came to discover the allusiveness of the delusion which culminated in a disconcerting realization—that this problem was ambiguous. Its very existence depended on invisibility. To make matters worse, the human being, fueled by this monster, became the monster and inevitably projected the monster. It was trapped in its own creation.

In searching for its hiding places, I found the light to be its specialty, and the dark its scapegoat. This is not the kind of light that illuminates the way, rather, it is directed into the eyes of the beholder, blinding them from the path. Here, the modus operandi is deception, delusion, and the manipulation and control of the body—a coup d'état on evolution, a protest the natural, a Spiritual Conspiracy.

We have been led to look in the wrong direction. We have been bamboozled, beguiled, betrayed. We have been cheated for far too long. We have been led to believe our enemy lies "out there." We have been led to "believe." Our plight lies in the emotional investment of our identification with the image.

I predict an awakening on this planet of epic proportions, where the realization of this conspiracy will spring to life. I see the long-hardened road of religious and spiritual delusion coming to an abrupt end, like a domino effect, cascading across the globe. Our species is angry on a deep level. We know something has been wrong for a long time. We are tired of being thrown the scraps. This is primal, guttural; the scream of an exhausted humanity who will not take no for an answer. They refuse to be duped any longer. It is the voice of reason and the shout of change!

Part 4 | The Great Delusion

Chapter 12

THE NEW PREJUDICE

"Prejudices, it is well known, are most difficult to eradicate from the heart whose soil has never been loosened or fertilized by education: they grow there, firm as weeds among stones."
— Charlotte Brontë

"If someone is able to show me that what I think or do is not right, I will happily change, for I seek the truth, by which no one was ever truly harmed. It is the person who continues in his self-deception and ignorance who is harmed."
—Marcus Aurelius

Prejudice has a dark legacy in the history of humanity from white supremacy and anti-Semitism, to sexism, caste, age, gender, disability, religion, language and nationality.

The word "prejudice" comes from the mid-15th century, meaning "to injure or be detrimental to." Other meanings are "contempt, injustice, prior judgment and even injury and physical harm." It appears that the word points to preconceived ideas that are not based upon fact. It is belief without basis. The judgments made exist in the mind of the person or group making the accusations. They are Subjective leanings, not scientific observations.

There is a world of difference between prejudice and informed activism. Prejudice is the lazy man's activism. It offers satisfaction of personal bias without the effort of objective research. It is more of an "unfavorable feeling" than an educated decision. In the case of Catholicism, where children are being molested, prejudice does not apply, for there is ample evidence for advocating judgment. With that in mind, I will explain prejudice as it applies to the human primate from the ideology of spiritual dualism.

The human primate has a long history of suppression and prejudice. Religion and spirituality have treated the mortal animal with disdain. Whether it is called "the man of sin," "the vessel of spirit" or the "fallen creature," primates have been forced to deny their native drives and judge themselves as inferior to the invisible self. *I assert that the hidden prejudice of our day lies in the denial of our evolutionary origins which reveals the bigotry toward the human primate.*

Tell the average person that they are a primate and you're most likely going to see a raised eyebrow or disconcerted expression. Try to start a discussion about sex, body parts or natural impulses, and the conversation will turn sour or comical. It isn't that we won't talk about these things, but that there lies a subtle disdain for the physical, as if we were distanced from our primate self in some way. It is as if there is a little person in the head, who peers through the eyes upon the body, like a master controller.

The split created by dualism has created a prejudice toward the human primate. From dancing monkeys in side shows to caged apes in our zoos the disconnection of our evolutionary past can be found throughout our culture. People are so busy seeing themselves as supernatural beings or icons of admiration that the thought of lowering themselves to the level of an ape is degrading.

The removal of bodily hair is obsessive in our culture, to such a degree, that an unshaven appearance is deemed unacceptable. Back and neck hair shares a common disdain as does the bearded face. The prejudice toward the human animal feeds the fantasy self to such a degree that it will do anything to maintain an almost alien appearance as in the case of fashion models. My point is not to protest shaving, but to address the bias against the furry upright animal.

The treatment of the body using drugs and alcohol are another symptom of this split. Bars and nightclubs are filled with humans who dump poison down their throats, recklessly abandoning the biology from which they drink. The unconscious disregard of the physical permits the person to treat "their body" like a vehicle that's been trashed without consequence. Unbeknownst to them, they are caught in the illusion of an invisible self who flaunts its superiority over the fleshy vehicle. Of course, this does not apply to the casual enjoyment of personal vices but does speak volumes of the wonton neglect (through mindless chemical abuse) that is prevalent in our society.

Not only does the split-mind find an excuse for harming the body, but this dangerous logic applies to other bodies. This can be seen in the culture of crime, where humans are treated like pieces of meat by the deranged. The ultimate violation is found in the horrifying acts against the innocent as in the case of child molestation, torture and human trafficking. The sex trade is at an all-time high, using the young as objects for the invisible predator who has hijacked the biology of the perpetrator.

You can also observe this prejudice in our language. During the early years of my spiritual quest, I paid special attention to the power of words. I was led to believe that the bible was the "Word of God," so, like any rational unenlightened person, I made every effort not to go past a word I did not understand. Having been indoctrinated as a Christian from birth, it came as quite a surprise when I discovered the contradictions, the violence and the fantasy of the holy writ.

Scripture is filled with dualistic language. In the account of man's origins, there are Adam and Eve, God and the Serpent. (Sounds like a sitcom) There are the physical elements and the unseen "cause" in the sky. The story of god and man progresses throughout the Old Testament demonstrating superiority over the corporeal by genocide toward man. In the New Testament dualism becomes much more personal, the body is reduced to that of flesh, and the soul it's dweller. The biblical story of the invisible god and spirit has maintained a hold on the minds of humans who have fallen prey to this dialectal prejudice. Our language is filled with support for this creature. A disdain for the physical is woven into common communication. The duality is validated by the unwary—subtly initiated by the invisible ghost.

Our schools are filled with teachers who explain away terrible events (as in the case of a child's death) by assigning the biblical story as an explanation. As innocent as it may seem telling a child that "Bobby is in heaven with Jesus," alienates them from the real world. The same happens with the belief in reincarnation where the afflictions of life are explained away by the belief in karma which glares in the face of humanity through the poverty in India.

Children need to "get" life for what it is so that they have time to integrate the natural world with all its ups and downs. As they grow into adults they need to understand the world they were born into, not the one that exists in the imaginings of their caregivers. Teaching fantasies through religious and spiritual stories only pushes off the inevitable reality of our world. The mid-life crisis could very well be a result of this careless disregard for the natural.

The New Prejudice - 121

In Arthur Koestler's book "The Ghost in the Machine" (published in 1967) the Cartesian model of dualism is challenged by his theory of the brain. Koestler explains that our brains are complex structures, and as they have evolved, they have built upon earlier more primitive parts. The human primate not only has the creative capacity of the frontal lobe, but the primitive layers that can overpower rational logic. Emotions such as anger, hate and lust—the kind humans either deny or explain away—are the regions of the deeper parts of the brain from which our vast array of creativity (via the frontal lobe) draws from. In other words, you don't get the fantastic imagination of a modern-day human without the primal brain structures that built it.

It is not hard to notice, once this is understood, how the dualistic story pales in comparison to the science of the brain. The primitive brain structures fall under the category of "the body, the flesh, the sinful man and negative energy." The higher brain structures are what are referred to as "god, spirit, consciousness and higher vibration." The spiritualist puts the focus on their imagination (crediting non-physical sources) while failing to truly understand the real source. Because of their identification with their cherished fantasy they unknowingly become the voice box for delusion.

The scientifically unenlightened ecclesiastical leaders of our past explained what we now know as "evolutionary brain development" in the narrow band of mythological stories. However, even in the glaring light of current science, the human animal continues to confirm its susceptibility to illusion. It requires an unfettered application of blind certainty to hold onto a belief in a non-corporeal entity, where no evidence exists, and at the same time overlook the voluminous data of evolutionary biology. Reason can only conclude that the plight common to all—is human frailty.

Statements such as "my body" imply ownership, yet, the average person does not realize the disassociation that occurs in their consciousness. Furthermore, the illusion of an entity that is "in command" feeds the primate body with all manner of ego-driven behavior. Objectifying one's self from one's body can have profound psychological effects. Thoughts are empowered as "things" and the material world is invalidated as illusion or experiential vehicle. This split lies at the root of a myriad of psychological problems ranging from narcissism to schizophrenia. There is evidence for inherited genetic memory that may play a significant role in the spread of this biformity which I encourage the reader to explore.

These effects of dualism can be seen in how we look upon nature like a picture on a wall. Humans visit the country on their weekend jaunts much like a tourist in a foreign land, when, in fact, the place visited *is* their "*natural ground of being*." The zoo is a classic example of the Disneyland type mentality distinctive of modern humans. Furthering the illusion are the cartoons fed to our children throughout their formative years where the natural is irreverently flaunted and distorted into talking animals—thus retarding the *actual* in the young mind of the natural.

It is my opinion that teaching a child dualism before they have developed a cognitive understanding of life is child abuse. Like the preacher or guru who believes they have the right to educate humanity because of a "special" Subjective experience, so the parent grossly assumes their self-comforting belief upon the child without understanding the repercussions. In fact, the belief-invested parent is most likely to defend their right to "train up a child in the way it should go" with a vicious righteousness.

The New Prejudice - 123

This unconscious prejudice toward the natural maintains its position by creating irrational confidence in the Subjective. We learn through our life experiences. It is in the actual physical world that we test our Subjective certainties. The imaginings of a child naturally develop into adult creativity rather than delusional fantasy, not by unchallenged beliefs, but by discovering the difference between *earned life experience and easily acquired fancies*. The religious and spiritualist have one primary thing in common, and that is the unquestioned confidence in their Subjective imaginings.

Unlike the rest of their species, they believe their brand of dualism gives them the unique right to assert their Subjective fancies on others without submitting to the test of critical questions. Thus, the invisible self maintains its existence behind mental walls that refuse to be penetrated while asserting its authority from the unconscious pool of assumptions.

We are one indivisible whole, not compartmentalized things, where phantoms control our bodies like machines. We are not looking "through" our eyes—we "are" the primate—seeing. The ghost in the machine has been found in the brain. The evidence leads to our evolutionary biology. Spiritual claims can be explained by natural means. The person new to these discoveries can find solace in the demonstration of this fact rather than the unending chase after the carrot of the unseen.

We need the *permission to be human* on a planetary scale. The prejudice toward the human primate only serves to keep our species in the dark ages. The subversion of the natural—piously degraded through the language of dualism—grants the illusion of bodily ownership. The truth that screams out against the spiritual imposter is the voice of humanity claiming its rightful place.

Spirituality is the shadow of the real.

Chapter 13

DENYING THE NATURAL

"Spiritual life is the bouquet of natural life, not a supernatural authority imposed upon it. The impulses of nature are what give authenticity to life, not obeying rules from a supernatural authority."
— Joseph Campbell

"God did not create nature, nature created us, and we created the idea of god which singlehanded destroyed nature."
— Diego Kricek Fontanive

By now, I'm sure you have figured out what name I give the infamous Ego—The Invisible Self. I have stated earlier in this writing that this *self* is nothing more than a reflection in one's imagination. It can take on whatever form as long as it remains in command of the organism. Any face will do, good or evil, hero or victim, saint or sinner—all are masks for this delusional entity. In the spiritual application, it carries a brand of deception that puts nature and the body in a subordinate position to an invisible soul or force. It is this type of thinking that fosters a denial of evolution and the natural world.

When you dispel the religious story, you are left with a gap that is commonly filled with some form of spirituality. Here, you have dualism with a new face, a soulful, holistic, non-religious appearance. There is the oneness of all religions, the unity of all faiths, and the mysterious spiritual energy from the soothsayers of pseudoscience. You see, when I got to this point, it wasn't so much that I knew I wasn't a Christian any more, but rather, that I had found a new *image of freedom* to attach myself to. This freedom was short lived because I began to see the same old religion wearing a different mask. New-Age spirituality is just a kinder, gentler version of this and in some ways more cunning—the wider the smile on this island—the subtler the denial can be. New Age-ism is filled with erroneous ideas about reality, seemingly innocent, but deceptively dualistic.

The spiritualists deny the evidence of evolution and objectify the body in a kinder and gentler way. The phrase "my body" has a sophisticated feel to it. It hails a trendy banner of Yoga and holistic practices. Soulful eyes sanctioned by the masters of the Far East mark the territory for the spiritualist and their beliefs, claiming superiority over nature while denying the human primate.

The body is reduced to a vessel to be channeled through by whatever masks the invisible self wants to wear. Spiritual teachings roll off the tongue of the master amazing the gullible seekers whose criterion for truth is whether it "feels" right or not. The channeling human conduit sits in defiance of evolution while claiming unseen virtues through the vessel being "used." The objectified carcass is paraded in front of the followers like a corpse hung out to warn the passersby not to question the smooth words of the orator. This of course is always done under the banner of loving feelings and hallowed truths. Truths so sacred that to question their validity may initiate a public scolding or joke at the expense of the inquirer. Innocent as it may appear, the dualism is reinforced by the collective amusement.

Just like the religious, spiritualists have a slippery way of beating around the bush and dodging reality. Their tactics are the same old game with a different slant. Their love is based on their beliefs—not on natural intelligence—which is born of the sacrifice of life. It is quite easy to discover the validity of the soulful appearance by asking the right questions. Find a spiritual person who oozes a bright aura of enlightenment and ask them if you may pose a few questions. If you know what you are doing you will know what to ask in order to get them "thinking." If thinking becomes too strenuous for them, you will most likely receive a number of reactions that appear less than spiritual. Open mindedness becomes rather closed when challenging the beliefs of the esoteric love slave.

However innocent it may appear; the spiritual person promotes anti-natural beliefs and does so with a smile. The arrogance is so strong that to point out a scientific fact, in disagreement of their reverie, may result in being accused of having negative energy. Radical inquiry is not allowed because to do so would disarm the phantom *craving*.

Ignorance grows in an environment where uninvestigated feeling fuels the spiritual hallucination. What is not understood by these believers is that *they are recovering the right to possess their childhood fantasies without being shamed for it*. Therefore the defense mechanisms are strong.

The denial of nature can be witnessed by observing the spiritualist and their offspring. Statements such as "old soul" and "reincarnated spirit" plant the seeds of dualism in the child's mind. Many times, the child will appear to validate these hopeful claims by use of their creative imagination. Genetic tendencies are replaced with dualistic suggestions that fly counter to the human primate and its evolution. These seeds split the young mind into the fake world of the self-indulgent parent.

Love, caring, nurturing and guidance are not the property of spiritualism, but the effects of biology. These are characteristics that have been earned over time. For example, true "human sacrifice" does not hang on a cross in a public display of divine sadism. Rather, it is the effort of life surviving in a species. Religion hijacks the real. It robs natural altruism from our species and replaces it with grace. Credit for the best in Homo sapiens is reassigned to the divine ego which has made every effort to mark its "territory," worldwide with its army of faithful followers and their castles of enlightened doom.

Dualism teaches the believer to distrust their darker emotions. They are so busy trying to "be" spiritual that they discount what is actually happening. Negative thoughts and feelings are the message reality is trying to present to us. I don't care how spiritual a person claims to be, if they are denying their shadow and replacing it with a light and love fantasy, then they are just as deluded as the orthodox religions from which they claim to have transcended.

> *Followers of the Way [of Chán], if you want to get the kind of understanding that accords with the Dharma, never be misled by others. Whether you're facing inward or facing outward, whatever you meet up with, just kill it! If you meet a Buddha, kill the Buddha. If you meet a patriarch, kill the patriarch. If you meet an Arhat, kill the Arhat. If you meet your parents, kill your parents. If you meet your kinfolk, kill your kinfolk. Then for the first time you will gain emancipation, will not be entangled with things, will pass freely anywhere you wish to go.*[1]
>
> —Linji

I have learned that my imaginings do not always line up with reality even if they are laced with good intentions. Consider, for a moment, how denying the natural creates a plethora of excuses in contrast to the real world. Natural feelings such as anger, jealousy, and fear, are pronounced unfavorable in the presence of higher consciousness. Human problems become the property of the accused who must realize the misuse of their godly powers. Nature is celebrated as the poster child for the supernatural, when, in fact, it is nature that created the brain that makes these claims. It is like we are stuck in our self-made costumes.

From the viewpoint of a human primate, a healthy sense of jealousy is natural. But from the viewpoint of the spiritual, jealousy is regarded as "negative energy" which places it beyond evolution into the divine realms from which the lie operates. Where natural growth and healing resolve the confusion of the wounded primate, spirituality distances the wound from the truth—because it is designed to deny the natural, submit the primate, and eventually kill its host.

Strong words? Just think about how many people go to their graves having never really lived, having given themselves entirely to the invisible, always interpreting the world through their "spirit goggles," frozen by fear, and caged in the doctrines of their belief. They denied their true feelings and bought a story to let them off the hook—they lived for the *afterlife* and threw away their *only-life*—neglecting the millions of unSpiritual moments that were screaming out to be noticed in their lives.

The natural world expressed through people, places, and things, reflected only empty shells for the divine while the problems of the world were either "left in God's hands" or attended to through the missionaries of the psychotic virus—enforcing the lie on the uninformed. The world missed the touch of one ordinary primate that could have made a difference, even if it was simply an honest hug. As Christopher Hitchens put it, "Religion poisons everything," and in my view, spiritualism does too.

Religious people do good things. They feed the hungry, help inner-city kids, aid victims of sex trafficking and contribute to others in need. I want to make a very important point here—religious people are human primates! They are doing what caring human primates do, but they're doing it under the guise of the religious story. Take away the story and humans still have the altruism in them that the religious experience hijacks. It is the natural world and our species that deserves the credit.

The funny thing about the word "delusion" is that it means just that—*delusion*. When you have it, you don't know it, and that can be a problem. In the quasi spiritual view, the lines between truth and fiction blend together into a smorgasbord of "other worldly" pleasures. No matter what angle you look at it from or how much you dilute it, the invisible imposter stays alive by shape shifting from one generation to the next. This contagion comes in all forms; you can see it glaringly in religion, cunningly in spirituality, and bubbling out of our everyday conversations.

Natural serendipitous events happen all the time for those who are open to seeing life without the conceptual "god goggles" on. I met a man at the coffee shop the other day who asked me if I would share my table with him. I agreed, and we both sat at the table working on our laptops without saying a word to each other. It wasn't until he got up to leave that we introduced ourselves to each other and briefly discussed our vocations. I came to find out that he was a professional photographer. At the time, I needed a profile photo for the unSpirituality project, and when he offered to do a photo shoot for free, I gladly accepted. Here was a qualified photographer, offering his professional services without any ties. He was just a normal guy who was happy to help me. Now, I could have easily spiritualized the event by adding all kinds of meaning. I could have said "I" manifested him," or "this is a sign of spirit guiding me." I could have told him that good things were coming his way because of his selfless act, but that seemed too contrived. The truth is, he was just a nice guy who loved his work and enjoyed doing random acts of kindness (he never mentioned spirit or religion). I was in the right place at the right time, and because I had prepared my website, I was ready for a picture—or the event would not have happened. Because he enjoys giving free pictures to random people, he most likely experiences random expressions of gratitude. Because of his outlook he positions himself in a receptive modality for serendipitous adventures.

Acting on a project that excites you places you in a position to see things that you would not have seen otherwise. Again, it's the yellow VW scenario where you decide you want to buy one, and from then on, you see them all over the place. That photographer probably has a lot of interesting and positive things happen for him because he "does" things for other people which in turn puts him in a position for more serendipitous events to happen. These events reflect what he is doing. Feed starving people and events will be "seen" that reflect that type of action. It is not a force "out there", but rather the human subjective, direction of movement and environment. It is a natural occurrence.

Associating with the contents of our brains creates fertile ground for a break in reality, meaning—that which is physical is not conceptual. In other words, a person's Subjective idea of a tree may not line up with the reality obtained through the senses of every human being on the planet. The tree might be experienced as someone's reincarnated grandfather, a strange alien creature, or a virtual construct. Our common reality—based on biology—reflects our shared human experience just as a knock on the head hurts no matter who you are. Just about everyone dies when they're shot three times in the head, and no one survives decapitation—it is just biology. Concepts about the natural that defy our common experience such as "the tree is a reincarnated dog because it barked last night" would be considered irrational in the context of our shared experience. Persons too confused about the outer world of the senses and the inner worlds of imagination are placed in homes for the mentally deranged to protect society. When you break from the physical, all manners of rationalizations appear in stark contrast to the natural world.

When it comes to the natural, our topic would not be complete without the mention of sex. Mention this word in conversation with others and prepare to see a multifaceted reaction. For some, sex is meaningful and natural and for others highly combustible. Somewhere in between lays a mixture of knowns and unknowns, fears, phobias and compulsions. Why is the one thing that is so vital to our existence tainted with bewilderment? It is the power house of emotion, the place from which we all emerge, and the playground of oceanic thrill.

In our denial, we have failed to understand this primate drive. We are surprised at the recurrence of broken relationships. If we had a healthy understanding of our natural impulses, would we be less careless in repeating the same mistakes over and over? Not unless there was an erroneous belief being adhered to—as in the case of finding one's "soul mate."

Admittedly, this is a novel idea, and engenders tenderness and a sense of deep love, but, I would argue that this is another ploy of the invisible self to hijack the natural. The idea of "soul mates" redirects the attention from the natural human being and its origins and places it on the spiritual story, which claims, superiority over nature. The deep connection between two people took millions of years to create and should not be assigned to a story that doesn't apply. When two people discover each other serendipitously, and end up becoming life partners, I see this as one of the wonders of our natural world, not the plan of an invisible androgynous inter-dimensional being who is balancing karma after being split in two many eons ago.

Sex is the domain of evolution not religion or spirituality. Sex has nothing to do with those traditions in the sense of its true assessment. Religion has boxed the *natural drive* into "marriage sanctioned before a judgmental god" and justified the mutilation of genitals as in the case of Jewish/Christian circumcision and FGM (female genital mutilation) which dates to ancient Egypt. It is a common practice among indigenous religions. (This should shine a new light for those who revere ancient Egypt and indigenous cultures as advanced enlightened societies).

While modern spiritual traditions have a more liberal and compassionate view of sex, the body is still seen as a "conduit" for spiritual energy. This latter point might seem trivial to some, but the implication of sex as a tool to climb up the spiritual ladder demeans the biology that created it. Why not view sex as a way for us to celebrate our humanity instead of pinning it to the spiritual poster board.

Of course, the spiritualists love to explore Tantra as a means to God realization, but I would argue that it is another dead end in the quest for the spiritual self. Intimate lovemaking is as natural as loving your child. There is no need to assign the spiritual quest to the process.

How one slices it up, biology dictates our sexuality and no spiritual ideology will cause that to change. We must get on with the program and begin to see life as it is. Only then, do we have a better chance to aligning with it rather than forcing it to be what we want. I am not saying that all persons that practice Tantra are denying the natural or not having deeply meaningful experiences, I am saying that the application of the invisible demeans the natural and takes the focus off the originator—which is biology.

Obsessions flourish where restriction and disassociation linger, especially when it is enforced with theistic, shaming ideology. *I am attempting to bring the human primate out from the Spiritual dungeon to which it has been sentenced into the light of natural beauty and tremendous talent— minus the esoteric dogma.*

The clergy may argue that they promote safe sex in the context of a married couple, but they never explain what to do with a born hermaphrodite. It doesn't make sense. Every time the "natural" whacks them in the face they come up with some lame orthodox excuse like, "God made them for a purpose" or "it is not for us to know why." Excuse me, does anyone have a blunt object in the house? —Oh My Ground, ridiculous! I've had two friends who were born both hermaphrodites and they suffered terribly at the hands of those who had no context in which to put them. Through surgeries and psychological torture, they tell a tale of survival in a culture suffering from scientific illiteracy and religious ignorance.

We have evolved enough over time to be able to decipher what is healthy and what is not. Sexual crime and dangerous excess do not reflect the activity of an intelligent human being. However, if you beat down, bottle, contain or conceal this precious gift, you will turn it into a silent monster. We get nowhere abusing a child or a pet so why would we think that our animal self is any different? Demonstrating respect will reciprocate respect. We don't force a flower to open, we simply water it. Sex, without intelligence is a gamble and human emotions are par for the course

What drives humans to be convoluted over this subject? It would be easy to assign religious teachings as the culprit, but I think that is just the beginning. I believe the outlaw in this rodeo is amnesia—cultural and global amnesia. It is as if we are on the planet of the apes and the apes don't believe they are apes. They are in love with an image of themselves and the spiritual story.

For thousands of years our species has been identifying with the divine image through religious and mythological stories which led to a total black-out of our evolutionary origins. This is big—real big—the kind of realized "Big" that comes along once in a millennium. This is not hard to conceive of once life is reviewed through the evolutionary lens. All that is required for the mental house of cards to come tumbling down is a little open-mindedness and an honest appraisal of the evidence.

I believe the denial of the natural reflects our cultural trance. This denial is enforced by the religious-spiritual dispensers of outdated wisdom. You would think we would be over this hurtle by now with the information highway rolling out of our computers like a runaway train. This problem goes much deeper and carries a price. *Keep your identity or suffer its death!* This requires brutal honesty!

The denial of the natural requires a relinquishment of identity, that is, the kind of identity that is excessively and compulsively fueled by emotion. No matter how irrational the teaching may be, if there is an emotional attachment, there is belief, commitment and defense. That we are still having debates on whether a two-thousand-year-old Jewish man arose from the grave or whether or not angel spirits and demonic entities exist, is alarming. What part of our natural experience lends itself to these speculations? There is nothing other than the phantoms in our brain, misinterpreted primal impulses, and the attachment to tradition that suggests that these things are real.

Have you ever seen a "real" physical miracle? Not the easy ones that can be explained. I'm talking about being right "there" while someone walks on water or levitates. Have you ever seen, with your own eyes, an arm grow out of a socket blooming fingers for a finale? Can we just, for once, ask one of these "finger pointing preachers" to part the pond outside the church? This will not happen because the evidence is Subjective and anecdotal. Therefore, the story continues while the blind lead the blind in a never-ending cycle of wishful thinking. No one in their right mind would ever plan their life around talking snakes, virgin births, levitating gurus, channeled entities, dead people walking on land or living people walking on water. It's crazy!!!

Admittedly, the natural world is filled with the pains of change either by natural disaster, human violence, suffering or loss. Our existence is not without birth pains and death. However, it is as it is, and making up stories to lull ourselves to sleep does not change the reality of life. We can educate ourselves and increase our understanding while dispelling much of the fear that plagues our minds.

Chapter 14

PLAGIARIZING NATURE

*"Enter, stranger, but take heed
Of what awaits the sin of greed,
For those who take, but do not earn,
Must pay most dearly in their turn.
So if you seek beneath our floors
A treasure that was never yours,
Thief, you have been warned, beware
Of finding more than treasure there."*
— J.K. Rowling

Probably the most blatant display of plagiarism, in all of history, is the spiritual story. The original work "Evolution" has been distorted and turned into the "unearthly story." Whether it is our evolutionary past, our speculative future or an emotion or idea, there is an invisible story to cover its natural explanation.

Early in my transcendent quest, I was caught one afternoon by a nature documentary. As I watched the film unfold I began to see that nature wasn't the Disneyland version I had been taught to believe through fairy-tales and Jesus stories. I was glued to the television, for hours, taking in a download of information that would foster new suspicions about my invisible enterprise.

There were some key connections I made at the time. The stories of the devil, demons, and dark spirits appeared suspiciously like the hunt and prey of our past. Piercing eyes, sharp teeth, claws, prowling and pouncing seemed a more accurate appraisal of the fears that haunt us than the silliness taught in the bible or the anecdotal stories of alien

Plagiarizing Nature - 139

abductions (that is not to say that they do exist, I don't know if that's the case, but the subjective fears in the wee hours of the morning reflect past trauma in most cases). Take the "monster under the bed" fear that children share around the world. Is it their imagination, a scary movie they watched, or the haunting of a ghost? Have you ever considered that the feeling of "being hunted" or "haunted" is in our genes? It is quite natural for young primates to feel afraid when "away" from their parents in a dark room. Primates need physical touch and never more desperately than when they're a child. It dawned on me that the spiritual stories were spawned from the natural world.

Another interesting observation I had was how incredibly deceptive nature appeared. Everything was trying to deceive everything else to survive. Beauty, scent, and similarity were used to allure prey into a trap, as is the case of certain carnivorous plants. The whole animal kingdom was one big manipulation factory for survival—but necessary for *growing* intelligent primates. This would offer up some more evidence for my growing suspicions.

I started making the connection between nature's "talent for deception" and religion and spirituality. It appeared to me that humans were doing quite well in this department. So well in fact, that they managed to convince their own species to believe in hidden worlds, with invisible characters, with the intent to fatten their survival and control others. When they discovered the power that a story wielded on their friends, religion was born. This allowed for control and management on a mass scale, by herding and corralling the apes, one story at a time.

The evolution of the world and its inhabitants has been turned into a non-physical landscape where invisible beings exist either in heaven, hell, or a dimensional plane. Like thought itself, the spiritual realm seems to profit under immediate manifestation in contrast to the natural world that requires time and effort to grow. The convenience of the metaphysical story makes it very alluring to the would-be-spirit-being; yet draws them into a make believe world that has done nothing other than to copy the original.

At the end of the day, it is biology that has the last word. Unfortunately, it is not given its proper due in the imagination of the oblivious. We are living in a time when arguments are being constructed in defense of an invisible Jewish man in the sky, who wears the badge of human sacrifice. This is still displayed in reverent awe on our television sets. The deception in this area is insidious. For example, the cunning denial behind the loving smile of the minister who "shares" his brand of orthodoxy to the public. I wonder if Darwin had higher hopes for our time.

However you dissect the spiritual story, it all leads to dualism and needs to feed to survive. In the new consciousness teaching, you find this infection everywhere. Bring in the Oprah's, Deepak Chopra's and the plethora of spiritual gurus who feed this denial through their particular brand of invisabilism. I will admit, however, that Oprah did a huge service to mankind by offering so many insightful perspectives on her show and many of the self-help gurus have provided much needed stepping stones for our species. In this writing, I am attempting to separate the wheat from the chaff.

I used to adhere to the belief, "I am a spiritual being having a human experience." This was the viewpoint I operated from for over 26 years. However, when I came across the realization of the natural, it made sense why this statement not only attracted followers but programmed them as well. Rising above the material world as a creator is a tempting proposition for humans. It dwarfs the mundane and opens unlimited possibilities. Why worship a god when you can "be" a god? I think opening one's mind to boundless possibilities is healthy, especially in light of the science of neuroplasticity (the brain's ability to reorganize itself by forming new neural connections throughout life). An open mind does not require delusional thinking or spiritual belief—just a sincere interest in exploring new vistas.

I believe our species is slowly waking up to their natural existence. For centuries, humans have believed they are special in a god's eyes—that the laws of nature don't apply to them. In their arrogance, they have built colossal cathedrals and amassed oceans of followers to make up for the invisible little tyrant in their heads. They have fought religious wars and stamped their unseen authority on the foreheads of their own species by the heels of their self-inflated boots.

In their denial, they have separated themselves from their earthly cousins with which they have grown and shared the tree of life. They have placed themselves above nature, in their orthodox conceit, and claimed oneness with the planet while denying the humanity it gave them. They pompously wear the garments of life through their beads, necklaces and anti-human garb, while judging others in their spiritual devoutness. They think they are so exclusive that they are above helping humanity (unless it is done in the name of their god or invisible force). The cop-out of otherworldly excuses is used to justify inaction while the world cries out for help. The spiritualists see themselves, in god's eyes, as being "called" from some non-human dimension. They are in love with the divine image of themselves.

Another example of plagiarism is how the New Age community plagiarized the Native American traditions. The divine narcissist does not care where it gets its food, it will take from anyone and anything.

The indigenous tradition is what I call an organic-Subjective-genetic-tradition. Subjective jewels passed down through generations that were culled from the slow and natural evolutionary continuum of a people and their environment. Their stories are as old as the land from which they came and carry priceless inner tools for the survival of their descendants. To make the point, I will include a quote from a Native American woman named Nora who makes her case against the "thoughtless" acts of the feel-good New Age community.

> "I would like to offer my views on this issue of Native American beliefs and new age beliefs. I am a Cherokee woman. My Mother was Nora Emory, the daughter of Sarah Willis, whose mother was a member of the Wolf clan of the Eastern Cherokee. What my grandmother taught me about the beliefs of the people are as opposite from the new age beliefs as anyone can get. Because the differences between the two systems, there is no way that there can be any merging of the two, without one group giving up their basic fundamental beliefs and adopting the other's beliefs. I am not willing to give up what my grandmother taught me. NO! THE NEW AGERS DO NOT DO A GOOD JOB OF REPRESENTING THE BELIEFS OF MY PEOPLE. They steal the ceremonies and parts of the beliefs that they choose, without permission, without knowledge. They bastardize them and re-package them for sale

> to the public either for money or credibility. And I am so very sick and tired of it. *What the new agers do to our beliefs is another form of genocide that my people have had to endure.*[1]

The sad part about this is that it reveals the desperation of the westerner to bring meaning into their lives. It is the portrayal of a saga where western man has been cut off from their human roots and trapped in the Gregorian calendar of religious ideology. It is evident that human biology is screaming through the constructs of the dualistic prison. It is an example of a generation who is hollow inside. Their hearts are empty, alienated from their ancestral connection, trapped in the constructs of modern industry, and blinded to their evolutionary origins.

In this dry land, divine arrogance waves the flag of invisibility while standing on the podium of nature. Their primate brain is denied and yet used, to promote the delusion. They spread the spiritual virus with a smile yet are totally self-indulgent in their quest for spiritual superiority—the kind of loving control the invisible self is all about. As long as it stays intact it does not care which mask is worn as it continues to assert superiority over the natural from which it is made.

Chapter 15

DIVINE NARCISSISM

"A narcissist is only interested in what reflects on her. All she does or experiences is seen as a reflection of self. The name of this psychological aberration is derived from the ancient Greek myth of Narcissus, a beautiful young man beloved of the nymphs. The nymph Echo fell in love with Narcissus's beauty, but he paid no attention to her increasingly mournful cries. To the Gods looking down upon the play of men, unrequited love was a crime. They punished narcissus in appropriate symbolic form by causing him to fall in love with his own reflection, ever reaching out to embrace an illusion. Each time Narcissus reached for his adored image mirrored in a pool of still water, it would dissolve into numberless ripples. The Narcissus, who is constantly trying to repair her injured self-esteem by adorning and admiring her gilded self, is also haunted by the terror of psychological fragmentation should she become aware that this self is not all she claims to be."
— Elan Golomb

"If Religion were true, its followers would not try to bludgeon their young into an artificial conformity; but would merely insist on their unbending quest for truth, irrespective of artificial backgrounds or practical consequences."
— H.P. Lovecraft

Narcissism is the modus operandi of the ego. It is associated with selfishness, vanity and conceit. It is not a word anyone wants to be associated with because of the self-inflated delusion it refers to. Even so, in pondering this word, I found that it fits the description of the "spiritual self" more accurately than its typical reference. It could be said that the nymph, Echo, represents the natural world and Narcissus represents the human primate. Upon rejection of the material world, the split occurred in the mind of the primate and it became enamored with its invisible self.

In the case of spirituality, narcissism takes on a much grander expression. The person is not simply in love with a positive image of self (or a negative one), but they are completely identified with "who they are" as something separate from the body. It is not simply an ego syntonic personality trait (consistent with one's ideal self-image), but the entire world is turned inside-out in service to this invisible self. A more accurate correlation would be that we live from the inside out through our subjective environment.

In the religious tradition the narcissist is identified with the god as in the case of Christianity where the scripture states, *"And raised us up with Him, and seated us with Him in the heavenly places in Christ Jesus."* This is a complete reversal of all things natural. The believer identifies with the glorious biblical images of themselves and their god. The normal world is fallen under judgment, and the human body is infested with sin.

The arrogance behind the caring eyes of the faithful leaks out when they perceive that their god is placing judgment on others. Everything in the divine narcissist's world is viewed through the lens of their all-knowing god and the spiritual image of themselves in his or her care. To keep this circus going the saved are instructed to read the bible daily, go to church regularly and have faith, while the esoteric lovers play catch with semantic meanderings. Anything that contradicts god's holy word is wrong. In other words, they are ordered to recreate nature to fit the biblical story and deny any physical evidence contrary to their belief. This sounds like narcissism on steroids.

With spirituality, narcissism puts on a different face. Nature is redesigned to fit the spiritual self and its discarnate domain while the physical world is conformed to the grandiose imaginings of the believer. Love is a "higher" domain that comes *through* the human vehicle to touch others. Negative feelings come from lower planes of existence, rather than their appropriate location—*the primal regions of the brain.*

Divine narcissists believe they are "special," and in their sweetness (and sweet they are), they put on a show for all to see. They are the poster children for the sacred and the fashion statement for the mystical. In some cases, they are the nomads of existence, seeing themselves as pilgrims passing through the earth plane.

For the pilgrims, humility is demonstrated through their supposed "selfless" lifestyle, yet, they feel privileged enough to assign their "presence" or their 'special knowledge" as their only duty to mankind. Of course, it is anyone's right not to do as they choose, but in the case of the spiritual pilgrims, they feel "called" or "chosen," and thus, they do not believe they are meant to be on the same level as the rest. The divine nomad feels "entitled" as if everybody's purpose was to oblige their path. In their false pride, they do not feel it is their mission to help other people in the world (the kind that requires selfless effort, care, or raising money, etc.), instead, the spiritual nomad sits in the sacred temple of "self" for all to see, stealing the light of real humanitarian efforts without getting dirty. The delusion is so strong that they feel their thoughts alone are sufficient to change the world for the better. It is a gross distortion of what is required to cause a change in the world. The invisible self is insidious.

The "goddess" is another example of divine narcissism where nature is exalted in her spiritual smile. She represents the earth, the mother and the divine. She is the arbiter of wisdom, the source of all life. She is in her power as the mother of all creation—which includes men! As beautiful as that may sound, the goddess is another image unto which humans identify. The arrogance of the invisible fosters super-human imaginings. These fantasies can range from the belief that she is "representing the earth" to "She is the vessel of the divine gnosis" (mystical knowledge). It is the same god-game but tailored for the female. Men in this story are considered "servants" of the goddess, worshiping her with adoring, reverent awe. She is a sign post for the invisible feminine. Once the "goddess goggles" are removed, the female primate becomes the glorious creature that she naturally is without the help of the spiritual story. Male primates do what is natural by treasuring the beauty of their opposite. Unfortunately, the narcissistic goddess adorns herself with nature while promoting dualism. This is the very ideology that places nature second to the spiritual delusion.

Divine narcissism can be repulsive to the natural person because of the aura of "knowingness" that is flaunted around. You cannot believe in a grandiose version of yourself with the creator of the cosmos without feeling a bit "more special" than others who are not in the "know" or the "now." It is almost impossible to hold the belief that the entire universe is created by your thoughts (including the people in it) and not suffer from some form of overconfidence.

When it comes to manifestation, it is rare (if not non-existent) that actual money is granted by the teachers of manifestation. In fact, in the 26 years of journeying through the metaphysical landscape, I can hardly remember a time that these divinely powerful creators could demonstrate their talents by manifesting money for others. I realize that teaching a person to fish is the best gift one can give; however, one would think that the divine spirit would have this one down and maybe splurge a little bit. I have received all manner of input from others about manifestation, but when it comes down to it, they conveniently assume that their advice is adequate proof for their powers. Just because a so-called new age teacher has an audience to ramble to about mystical powers, does not make them any different than the Christian faith healer who does the same. The saying, *"give a man a fish, and you feed him for a day, teach a man to fish, and you feed him for a lifetime"* is not difficult to understand and can be intuitively applied without superhuman powers.

The invisible self is so cunning that it attributes all the problems in the world to the choices of spiritual beings totally denying the effects of the natural world and the vulnerabilities of human mammals. It is an egoistic power trip used to invalidate ordinary humans by holding them to a supernatural standard. If a volcano erupts and kills an entire tribe the spiritualist will say that the villagers created the event. I think it is the worst case of hypocrisy to come "in the name of love" and believe such narcissistic poison. The divine narcissist adorns their "temple of self" without lifting a finger to help humanity unless it feeds their spiritual agenda. Again, all of this is another mask for the same old religion.

The fondness the divine narcissist feels for themselves and the universe is far more important than the feelings of "other" people. They might offer a "session" to help someone find a spiritual solution, but basic human assistance is off the table. If another person's plight begins to "lower" their energy, they will retreat to a safe place. Their imagined invisible guides can then comfort them with signs of approval for their act of *courageous self-love*. Giving good advice and helping others in need does not require supernatural assistance. I think people are afraid to just be human and trust their own natural wisdom. Again, let me preface here. Of course, I am stereotyping under the spiritual banner and this assessment does not apply to every person who believes in spiritual matters, but, the description has a place in the metaphysical field and I think it needs to be put on the table. Not everyone who offers sessions lacks altruism.

Divine narcissists are not the mouthpiece for the natural or the harbingers of truth that they sincerely believe themselves to be. The confidence with which the smiley spiritualist blindly flaunt is their own undoing. The reality of the natural world will defy even their most cherished beliefs. Imagining oneself as a divine being does not make a person any less primate, rather, their susceptibility to delusion adds another feather in the neurological cap.

Chapter 16

OBSESSED WITH THE INVISIBLE

"I worry that, especially as the Millennium edges nearer, pseudoscience and superstition will seem year by year more tempting, the siren song of unreason more sonorous and attractive. Where have we heard it before? Whenever our ethnic or national prejudices are aroused, in times of scarcity, during challenges to national self-esteem or nerve, when we agonize about our diminished cosmic place and purpose, or when fanaticism is bubbling up around us – then, habits of thought familiar from ages past reach for the controls."
— Carl Sagan

"Religion is still useful among the herd - that it helps their orderly conduct as nothing else could. The crude human animal is in-eradicably superstitious, and there is every biological reason why they should be. Take away his Christian God and saints, and he will worship something else."
— H.P. Lovecraft

Why are we so obsessed with the invisible? Does not the thing seen demonstrate how life works? Can the garden be "beautiful" without the fairies? Is the leaf not appreciated for the natural thing that it has become through evolution rather than assigning it to an invisible counterpart? It is as if the natural world is just not good enough. There must be something undetected that justifies its existence. This problem can be likened to an addict who cannot stop using.

Obsessed with the Invisible - 151

The obsession with the invisible drives the mind of the dualist into a never-ending reach for the mirage.

Death cannot simply be the end of a life, but the beginning of the invisible self's adventure. Birth is not revered as the earned arrival of millions of years of evolutionary development, but the chosen vehicle for the spiritual being's proclivities. Nature is reformatted into non-material realms for the disembodied as if the natural world efficient enough. The sun, moon, and stars are seen (in current quantum spirituality) as a hologram, which we "powerful creators of reality" have designed.

I think the true explanation for our obsession is right behind our eyes. It is the subjective world in which we operate. It is the imagination and emotions, the dreams and nightmares, the internal images we have yet to truly understand.

I think our species is so tainted from the spiritualism pervading our culture that we feel a need to assign an invisible "cause" to just about everything that amazes us. The beauty of a smile, sincerity and compassion, sunsets, hummingbirds, kindness and intuition all must be the work of the spiritual story. Assigning unbounded imagination to nature is the magic of life, but that is not the same as crediting invisible forces. Our imaginations grew through many thousands of years and it is this function that allows us the experience of open-ended possibility. It is the best that our evolution offers because it gives us the experience of being alive and develops new ways for our brain to grow.

It is hard to get around the obsession with the invisible in our society. Just about everywhere you go there is a reminder. I received a piece of mail the other day from one of the local churches. The cover of the 6x9 post card read,

"Praise the Lord from the heavens; Praise Him in the heights! Praise Him sun and moon; Praise Him all stars of light!" Excuse me, did it ever occur to you people that your unsolicited advertisement was not only offensive, but an insult to my existence? On the back of this propaganda was the Master's Bible Church with the following statements of faith: *"We follow the one true and risen Master, the Lord Jesus Christ. We teach the Bible, Gods revealed truth to mankind. We are a Church, people gathering for worship & outreach."*

The Christian cult is probably the biggest elephant in the room for western society. From the pope to the peppered landscape of churches across continents, this delusion is spoon fed to us through the denial and defiance of reality. Insinuating that a "master" who has defied our common knowledge of natural existence is an entity that must be submitted to—under threat of hell—is an absurd proposition. That the "Lord" has a book which we must assume is the ultimate truth adds more insult to injury.

Another example of this is new age evangelism, such as, "The Ashtar Command." Here we have a supposed off-planet race that uses human bodies like television sets to communicate the teachings of spiritual evolution which is in contradiction to the culminated evidence of our biological origins. Biblical sources, such as "Archangel Gabriel," assume a stamp of authority on the alien scrolls. The spiritual story of the so-called Ashtar Command is another example of the lengths to which the invisible self will go to elicit attention. As long as the story remains in the non-physical world, it excites the obsession of the ill-informed.

Consider this. With all the spiritualists who claim to be receiving knowledge from higher dimensions, including alien entities and 35,000-year-old warriors (such as Ramtha), [1] why hasn't anyone submitted scientific

Obsessed with the Invisible - 153

knowledge that could dramatically enhance our civilization? I am talking about specific testable knowledge concerning earth and the universe that "stuns" the scholarly community. *"Instead, all we are offered are banal homilies."*[2] The imagination acts just as it should when the human primate intuits millions of years of evolutionary wisdom. It took eons to grow a brain and nervous system capable of exploring the universe as humans do.

The obsession with the invisible is held in tact by the subconscious command to "not look." Because the physical eyes and brain are demoted, asking a believer to "look" at the evidence is resisted. Some spiritualists, who are more open than others, might entertain a discussion of the topic, but will surely argue for the invisible to the bitter end, or lovingly disconnect from you. Their emotional identification will not allow the feeling of "no-self" to occur so the irrational dialog continues to the dismay of the genuine inquirer. If they were comfortable in their natural existence, the thought of "new discovery" would be a welcome treat.

Many times, the believer will turn the tables, in a desperate attempt to disarm the person who is presenting the facts, by suggesting they are close minded. In fact, "not looking" at evidence is a characteristic of a closed mind. The resistance expressed by the spiritualists proves their dilemma. *The sincere seeker of truth isn't worried about being wrong if it leads to truth.* A genuine desire to become educated is the hallmark of an honest student, but for the person suffering under the spiritual trance, the enthusiasm of learning turns into a struggle for identity.

The obsession with the invisible is the delusion of the closet primate. They will go to any lengths to validate their denial, even to the extent of misrepresenting scientific research. In the case of particle physics, the "observer effect"[1] is taken out of its proper context and inserted into spiritual philosophy. Just because waves and particles respond to the act of observation on a quantum level does not support the idea that the moon only appears when we look at it. The theories set forth in the science of quantum mechanics apply to the micro level, not the macro. It just does not work that way. But those obsessed with the invisible will grasp for any data that might validate their compulsive reach.

Science is exciting, it is curiosity on steroids. It is fresh and opens up amazing new possibilities for our existence. I am in favor of any science that opens up the doors to the unseen universe, but because I have observed so many false claims made by the metaphysical community, I am not interested in overlooking the details.

Pseudoscience hands the novice inquirer an easy route to so-called certainty and seemingly always shouts from a position distrustful of mainstream science (as if all these scientists are part of a coordinated effort to deceive mankind). As in the case of conspiracy theorists, critical thinking is not the order of the day, and their speculations must assume that a wicked oligarchy is running the world. Is it true that corruption exists? Do some corporations treat the environment with disdain? Arc some cops bad cops? Sure, but to believe that all people, in all governments, are part of one big evil conspiracy is to deny the very evolution that brought us to the remarkable world we live in. The real evil in the world is the pain living in the biology of the masses. We are adapting to our ever-changing environment and that entails mistakes on all levels, even with our smartest scientist.

Contrary to cynical demand, author and experimental psychologist, Steven Pinker reveals, in his best-selling book

"The Better Angels of our Nature,"[2] that despite the ceaseless news about war, crime, and terrorism, violence has been on the decline over long stretches of history.

It is common for the religious or spiritual to adhere to bad news on the "physical plane" because it supports their invisible story. Nevertheless, the truth is that we have evolved over the centuries. Our world is more enlightened than ever. Our global consciousness is a result of fantastic technologies—not the arrival of some mysterious consciousness. It required "brains" to make this happen and brains do not grow overnight. Science has produced medical breakthroughs, space travel, and remarkable communication technologies that bring our species together using cell phones and the internet. None of this happened through superstition, but by the dedicated research of living, breathing human beings.

The spiritual story obsessively usurps the authority of the natural world, like the flaming head of Oz, but is merely a figment of the biology behind the curtain.

Revelations of a Zombie

Hello, we are zombie. We have been around for millennia. We were sent here by order of the evolutionary continuum. It has been our job to awaken mankind to their human self.

In lieu of spirituality, we have presented the truth of your reality. You are animals and you always have been animals. Now, the word animal is an interesting word. It has been ostracized by the faithful as something vile, something to overcome, some "thing" evil, in need of correction. Yet animal is only a word that refers to a thing.

The word "animal" has been desecrated. It once represented your proud origins; it refers to a "living creature." It does not mean you are a zombie or a predator or a fallen being. It does, however, refer to your evolutionary origins. Please understand its meaning in Latin, *animale* means "living being; being which breathes." Is there any reason one would not be proud to don that title? I think not.

We knew, from early on, that mankind's evolutionary step in conceptualizing nature would one day come to an end. We also knew that it would become your undoing. The distance between your kind, reflects the separation you so believe. I tell you, life is self-evident, it *is* the creator of the mental image.

So, we arrived many thousands of years ago to remind you of your true nature.

You, oh human being, have lost your way. You have fallen prey to the projection of your psyche. You have forgotten who you really are and replaced the natural with your imaginings. You have believed in the story of creation handed down by the elders of denial. You gave your true self away in trade for provision and notoriety. For some, the self-betrayal was succeeded under force. You succumbed to the lie to protect your young . . . we understand . . . we truly understand.

We began this endeavor when notable figures could be broadcast to the masses through the written word. We quietly engineered the message through the stories of your iconic spiritual leaders. These chief conductors represented the image you were addicted to. They were lofty projections of your illusion. You were not ready to know the truth at that time, so the image provided a stepping stone from which you could climb to this current day.

Untainted by delusion, you fell in love with the story of your projected self. The invisible you, with its pre-birth story of reincarnation, the endless contradictions to organic life, and the terror of death were all necessary imaginings.

Your emotions were the key to this delusion. We knew that your feelings dictated your reality, because you grew out of the earth. The images that you adhered to, through deep emotional scars, sealed the deal for many thousands of years. Attempting to convince you that your imaginings were unreal would only strengthen your defense.

So we concocted a way to get your attention . . .

Subtle, yet in your face, we screamed out in the stories of your imaginings. We rose from the dead and walked the streets through the writings of the devout. We clawed our way into your living rooms to reflect your human origins. We stood on the heels of your predators to remind you of the chase. Yes, you forgot you were once preyed.

We are the loyal officers from the delegation of natural selection. We entered into your psyches subtly, yet profoundly . . . we got your attention.

I tell you, now is the time for you to see the truth. Your species has become infatuated with our kind. From the stories of your ancient past, up to the present enlightenment of your media, we have only mutated into myriad forms—different faces, but the same message - *you are PRIMATE!*

We now ask you to stand up and affirm who you really are. Be proud of your heritage. Stop bowing down to those still in denial and awaken your brothers and sisters to who they really are. Gone are the days of your slavery, gone are the days of bowing to the invisible imposter.

Arise and BE HUMAN.

Part 5 | Soft Landing

Chapter 17

NATURAL LOVE

"A low thrum in his gut. Love. What is the measure of such a thing? Love, or the word love, is like an elusive jungle bird that because it is so durable has thousands of mimics and camouflaged neighbors."
— Lawrence Krauser

"Love is the burning-point of life, and since all life is sorrowful so is love. The stronger the love, the more the pain. But love bears all things."
— Joseph Campbell

A discussion about spirituality would be incomplete without addressing love. It is the one feeling, above all, that defines the spiritual experience. Logic, thinking and rationality all come second to this transcendent feeling. It is this oceanic experience that gives rise to the stories we assign to it.

Is love the property of the spiritual realm? Is it an expression of some invisible force, spirit or god? Is there an organic explanation for this boundless phenomenon? I assert that love is the property of our biology and the natural world from which we came. Love is a strong emotion.

It is the domain of intimacy for the human primate. It is the feeling of awe, wonder and the affinity with nature. It defines us as human beings. It has evolved over long periods of time through intimate genetic connections with life on earth. It is the impulse of the life in which we *live, move, and have our being.*

In an article entitled "Biology of Love" by Humberto Maturana Romesin and Gerda Verden-Zoller, the essence of natural love is so articulately captured:

> As neotenic, sexual, tender, and sensual animals, we humans are loving animals that become ill when deprived of love. But at the same time, as languaging animals that live in conversations, we humans can reflect on our circumstances, and we can invent, and have invented, rational systems in the form of religious, political, philosophical, and economic theories, that we have used to justify our doings and the negation of our emotions. As we have done that during the last ten thousand years, particularly in our occidental culture, we humans have become alienated from our basic condition of loving animals, and we have begun to live through those theories the rational justification of the systematic and systemic negation of the other (love) through the defense of transcendental values, and rational or revealed universal truths. In the blindness that the negation of love creates in our living, we stop seeing ourselves as part of the harmonious interconnectedness of all existence in the unending dynamics of life and death, and we begin to live guided by ambition, greediness and the desire for control and continuous relational difficulties that open ended population growth and misapplied technology, in the belief that it is the

> solution to all our problems has brought to us, and we are not happy. Indeed, we suffer, because we become denied by the very same world and psychic existence that we are bringing about, as this is a world and psychic existence, that denies the fundamentals of our existence as loving animals.[2]

In the spiritualist camp, however, love is assigned to a special teacher, energy, force, consciousness or god. Love is such a profound feeling that, for the spiritualist, assigning it to the natural somehow lowers its significance. This is another example of denying, plagiarizing and hijacking the natural—giving credit to the invisible rather than the physical.

Love is the secret weapon that cults use to manipulate their prey. If you take a closer look into this phenomenon, you will find that the feeling of love and belonging is a major factor in the conversion process. It is the "light worker" or "minister of Christ" that uses love, alongside fear, like a carrot and a stick to corral the primate herd into cooperation.

Human beings are love-dependent, communal animals. To such a degree that we build ourselves churches, in order to fulfill our social needs. True to the tradition of denial, humans assign their fellowship to a "Holy Spirit" or "Spiritual Energy" instead of acknowledging mammalian emotion. I remember the "sacred" feeling of the "Holy" *spirit* in my Christian days and how surprised I was to find the same "felt" experience in metaphysical circles. They called it "Heart Energy," I call it *shared human feeling*—humans in proximity with each other feeling common biology.

The presumptuousness of the *loving* disciple reeks of divine arrogance to the natural human being. Case in point, the Jehovah Witness who comes to the door with caring eyes, assuming you are lost, without even getting to know you. By the mere fact of "not" believing as they do you are unworthy of their "getting to know you." It's either "their way or the highway." Not very loving now is it? They don't see how terribly snobby and presumptuous it is to come to someone's door and suggest that they are there to save you from the wrath of the creator of the universe. I find it humorous when I think of the scenario being turned around. I don't think they would be so happy if I were to knock on their door and attempt to convert them to the "Flying Spaghetti Monster."[1]

Sedona, Arizona, is known for being a new-age hot spot with all kinds of spiritual activities. Having lived here for over 16 years I have seen spiritual love expressed in many forms, sometimes very sincere and other times laced with divine conditions. There were times when I felt assaulted by the love gushing from the human conduit as if there was something wrong with me because I wasn't in the spiritual mood.

Honoring all emotions is something I value, and when I am having a terrible day, well then, I am having a terrible day. It doesn't make me any less spiritual than the next person. In fact, I would argue that being brutally honest with oneself about feelings of anger, resentment, hostility or depression is the most "spiritual' thing a person can do—rather than covering them up with positive affirmations.

Of course, now that I am unSpiritual, I have given myself *permission to be human*, so I don't have to measure my emotional state by that of an enlightened guru or god. Being truthful enough not to pretend to be happy and loving while feeling the opposite emotion is a great milestone in maturity. This does not grant a license to act out, but to be sincere and honest. *All emotions and thoughts arising in the moment of our experience are aspects of ourselves awaiting our curious inquiry—it is information from our biology, it is natural intelligence.*

A few years ago, I knew a man who came into the coffee shop every morning who flaunted divine love (with glowing eyes) as if he were an ambassador from unseen realms. He may have viewed himself as the local poster boy for loving energy, nevertheless, he made it a point to profess divine love to friends, acquaintances, and even strangers. Although some people do this sincerely simply because they are happy, this type of behavior raises red flags when it is attached to invisible realms other than the natural subjective.

One morning, while I was stirring my newly acquired Americano, he came up to me, with a big smile and dreamy eyes, and in rote fashion said, "Hey brother, I love you." I asked myself, "He says this every time he sees me, but is he really sincere? If so, what is it about me that he loves?" One would think that expressing love to another person (at the very least) would be derived from some conscious intent and thought. So I asked him, "What is it about me that you love?" His response was one of bewilderment at the thought of actually having to "think" about the question. His reply was typical of the divine narcissist. He said his "Higher Self" was responsible for pretty much everything, and that his mind was surrendered to this power, (something like that) pointing to the idea that he is imperfect and spirit does his thinking for him.

This, of course, lets him off the hook for having to admit that his *loving confession* wasn't really about me, but about his self-indulgent Spiritual obsession. Had he been sincere he would have answered the question and taken personal responsibility. Assigning a "Higher Self" for the cause of everything is a very convenient position to take as one can hide behind their higher power like a child hides behind his or her mommy or daddy.

The Higher Self is the energy of the biology functioning in real time. It is the natural evolutionary intelligence operating beyond the volitional "I" of the so-called individual. The human primate identifies itself as an imperfect creature who needs a Higher Power to help it through the day. In actuality, this is a negative self-image that is fueled by the notion of a *positive higher power*. It is a dualistic construct built to last until deconstructed through curiosity and insight.

The next thing I said to him was, "it sounds like an insult, too easy." I told him, "You say that to me almost every time you see me, you must have taken the time to ponder what you admire most about me." His reply was, "you are complicated." I replied, "well, is there anything else that you admire about me that compels you to announce your love publicly or are you simply gracing the environment with your divine presence?" His answer vaguely retreated into the "Higher Self" as being the responsible party in his life. In other words, "no," he was not being sincere and thoughtful with his compliment toward me. He was conveniently throwing one of the most important words in the human experience around like a rag doll. He felt entitled, because of his connection to the divine. He did not take the time to think about the attributes and characteristics that made him love me. He used love to attract attention to his invisible self.

He is at a stage on the path where the bright, beautiful, invisible-self reigns supreme. He is blinded by the light of his own spiritual beauty projecting outward toward others in an effort to have his divinity reflected back. It is the function of the image to feed off the attention of others to survive—because it isn't real. *It is a hallucination of the primate.*

Now, was this person sincere? Did he feel love deeply? I could assume yes, but in this case, I would lean toward self-indulgence rather than a thoughtful compliment. Was he using love to stroke his spiritual self-image by graciously endowing me with his Higher Self's love? It is unclear whether he really cares about me or the feeling he experiences when he says he loves me. It does appear that he loves to be "seen" by others in the spiritual light. If my suspicions are true, then I assert, that this is childish love. It is the child trapped in the psyche who is garnering all the attention it can from the people in its environment.

Because the divine narcissist puts themselves in such a high position, social interaction looks more like an audience for the dancing spiritual ego. Because of the perceived distance, the star of the show can do what they want without being held to the same standard as the crowd.

Being human has its ups and downs, but spiritualists want to live in a world where there are only ups, and that is why the spiritual story was created in the first place—to keep life on the "up". Yet, it is a dangerous proposition because in order to live positively all the time one has to hide, suppress, reject or project their painful emotions. It is a dualistic portal through which to view the universe. Painful and uncomfortable emotions are simply information and insight being presented by our biological experience. All subjective content is extremely valuable for our ever present and unique human expression. It is the stuff of artists, yet, the true art is the individual human being. There is a sense of contentment when a person accepts life on their own terms, there is no fighting or resistance to "what is," and the struggle to "always be happy" is released.

I have witnessed "the cosmic feeling of love" be used to elicit sex, attention, respect, food, water and shelter. Just like the Christian who is given special treatment because of their commitment to missionary work, so the spiritualist is "succumbed to" because of their "WOW-ness" factor of divine love. Add a beard and some yoga, a visit to India and a trendy spin-off from the teachings of Osho, and the love is flowing like drug money from a cocaine dealer.

The divine narcissist comes in all packages, from religion to yoga, meditation retreats and cults. Love, in most cases, is the key emotion that pulls people into cults such as "the Peoples Temple, Heaven's Gate, the Branch Davidians and the Moonies." Just because someone is intoxicated with love does not make their beliefs true nor does it release them from personal responsibility. It does not make their version of invisibility any truer than the next.

What this reveals is a trance state that makes them feel special, and thus, entitled to parade their spirituality in front of the world—*as if no unSpiritual person feels love this profoundly.* The truth is, many people feel love deeply, however they are not compelled to wear it on their sleeves for all to admire. Authentic love is real and does not need to validate its existence by drawing attention to it. Natural love does not hide behind a facade. It is not a thoughtless act or an unconscious feeling, it is the thoughtful actions of sincere, whole, individuals.

The new-age universe is filled with the *feeling* of love, but it is not the kind of love that gets dirty from self-sacrificing deeds. You will not see this type of love sacrifice its comforts for humanitarian contributions. In the 26 years of my spiritual path, I don't recall a time when I have witnessed self-sacrificing altruism by the "conduits of the divine" outside people like Gandhi and Martin Luther King. Aside from drum circles, sweat lodges, meetings with divine messengers and worshiping one's chakras in ambrosial adoration, there are no special endowments that separate the divine narcissist from anyone else in the world.

When it comes to *real* change, the altruistic acts of the average person come naturally. The worst hypocrisy is presenting oneself as a messenger of light while doing nothing to solve real-world problems such as crime, hunger, child abuse and poverty. Divine narcissism is extremely focused on the comforts and adoration of the spiritual self while claiming the unearned praise of humanitarian sacrifice. While this cosmic love adorns the spiritualist with delusions of unseen support and veneration, any efforts outside their "thoughts" to promote world peace are deemed unnecessary.

Real love comes "built-in" to the human organism. As humans develop, and depending on their experiences, their definition of love will change from self-orientated, to family, friends and ultimately their species. If they have only experienced the love of family, then they will most likely not understand the depth of compassion one feels in a refugee camp, or in a disaster relief effort. If a person has never raised a child, they do not understand the meaning of self-sacrifice. They do not know what it is like to suffer the early-morning feeding of their infant while simultaneously feeling tremendous love. This is true human sacrifice.

Of course, it would be absurd to consider that every person who subscribes to spirituality is a guilty of false love. Love means diverse things to people depending on their background, genetic disposition and experience. Beyond the "concept" of supernatural love lies the rest of humanity who can experience awe, wonder, depth, and oneness, from a sunset or a kiss without assigning the spiritual story or its "star self" to it. It is the expression of true humility and sensitivity within the natural world and its creatures.

Chapter 18

UNDERSTANDING THE SUBJECTIVE

"Folks, it's time to evolve. That's why we're troubled. You know why our institutions are failing us, the church, the state, everything's failing? It's because, um – they're no longer relevant. We're supposed to keep evolving. Evolution did not end with us growing opposable thumbs. You do know that, right?"
— Bill Hicks

"Pleasure to me is wonder—the unexplored, the unexpected, the thing that is hidden and the changeless thing that lurks behind superficial mutability. To trace the remote in the immediate; the eternal in the ephemeral; the past in the present; the infinite in the finite; these are to me the springs of delight and beauty."
— H.P. Lovecraft

For some, there is a typical response to the spiritual landscape once the blinders are taken off, and that is, to throw out the inner experience with the religious drug of choice. This is an unnecessary leap. Why allow the outdated descriptions of our human Subjective experience to be hijacked by the religious and spiritual tradition? Why not give credit where credit is due (biology/energy) and take back our inner world from the religious and metaphysical domains and define for ourselves the experience of our internal world.

My "coming out" of religion and spirituality eventually grew into a balanced perspective. I found that the tools I collected from metaphysics still served me quite well. I clearly understood the science of the brain and Subjective states. I knew the difference between pseudoscience and peer reviewed research and my internal universe became an even richer resource of information and inspiration. In fact, because of my new skeptical grounding, I gave myself more permission to play and experiment with the Subjective.

If I was suffering from financial issues I comforted myself by visualizing unlimited amounts of money in my possession to create the feeling of wealth, yet, I no longer assigned a spiritual dimension or godly powers to the process. Belief and identification were no longer necessary, rather, I was generating a "feeling" by the imagery. For me, synchronicity (as Carl Jung put it) is a common experience. Whether it is negative events or positive events, the current of life is constantly reflecting our subjective *feelings* and convictions.

Do we create our reality? Absolutely! But not in the way the extremist believes. We don't alter the laws of the natural world simply by thought—this is delusion—we do, however, alter our "experience" of the world with our subjective pallet. We are made of star dust, and it comes as no surprise that life can appear to magically unfold for the person who is in tune with their inner world. The magick of the esoteric traditions is really the genetic connection to all life on earth and our shared inner world is reflected upon ourselves through our experience. We can commune with nature because we *are* nature itself.

One field that is worthy of note is neuroplasticity or brain plasticity. It refers to how the brain changes with behavior, environment and bodily injury, and replaces the formerly held position that it is a static organ. The beauty of this science is that it opens new possibilities as to how our imagination affects the human experience—this points to the correlation between the environment and biology morphing in real time—like evolution slowed down to just above static. Simply put, your outlook on life, in conjunction with the environment, creates a chemical reaction which can lead to either a healthier or a less than desirable existence.

The "create your own reality" philosophy can be twisted into a multitude of erroneous assumptions to fit the comforts of belief. It is important to decipher the difference between delusional thinking and subjective creativity. Creating one's reality does not include turning a tree into a dog or making the moon disappear. It does mean that we have an amazing ability to interact with our environment through our inner world.

When we focus on certain ideas, the thought "to see" these ideas reveals them in our environment. These things do not appear out of nowhere because they were *thought* into existence. Simply put, they were already there and now they are seen. So, think about crows, and you will "see" crows everywhere (or at a very special moment). Now, try to think about something that is *not* available in your immediate environment such as the space shuttle. The next time you see the space shuttle in the newspaper, on television or on the internet, you will have an exciting feeling of "aha," so long as the intention is remembered. It could be weeks, or months, but when the image of the intended thought appears, the connection is made. I don't get as surprised as I used to as it has become a natural occurrence in my life.

Exploring the Subjective can be a very slippery slope. Humans are very prone to certainty, which is one of the primary seeds of belief.

Neurologist Robert Burton, in his book On Being Certain,[1] explains the following:

> Despite how certainty feels, it is neither a conscious choice nor even a thought process. Certainty and similar states of "knowing what we know" are sensations that feel like thoughts but arise out of involuntary brain mechanisms that function independently of reason.

This is pointing to the fact that humans have a biological need to assume certainty based on our evolutionary development. He goes further in chapter 9:

> If, through snap judgment or insightful deliberation, you avoid a charging, hungry lion by scurrying up a tree, you have concrete evidence of the value of your thoughts. The lion slinks away and settles on gazelle tartar for lunch. You climb down from the tree feeling that you have learned something. The feeling of knowing and the decision to climb the tree become linked together in the neural network labeled "what to do in case of a charging lion." The more powerful the experience and the more times it occurs, the greater becomes the linkage between the decision and the feeling that the decision is correct.

Because of how we are wired our tendency to be certain about our Subjective experiences without testing their validity can create a sea of assumptions. These assumptions are the beginnings of belief in irrational ideas which cause one to defend them as if they were real. Michael Shermer states in his book, "The Believing Brain:"[2]

> An uncertain and doubting mind leads to fresh world visions and the possibility of new and ever-changing realities.

Being grounded in a practical understanding of science and critical thinking is a great way to explore the internal world without getting lost. I also recommend the Focusing[3] method which will be explained in a following chapter.

My advice to believers in the supernatural is to have some fun experimenting with manifestation by testing the limits on the popular methods. For instance, test how long it takes to manifest a red apple versus how long it takes for a new car. Explore immediate manifestation like a phone call from a friend or a weather balloon landing on your house. Take a trip to the middle of the desert, where there are no chances of human interaction or access to commodities and see if you can manifest a veggie burger. Put metaphysics on the chopping block and see what it's made of—have fun breaking rules and creating new ones. Challenge supernatural powers, consider the available brain science, and see what results come about.

The child must grow up and suffer the disappointment of the tooth fairy's non-existence. No matter how much they muster up the belief, the tooth fairy still does not exist, and the chances of becoming the president of the United States next week are quite slim. Unfortunately, believers distort natural logic, they twist their Subjective reality to make it appear as though their wish came true. Unfortunately, even though magical experiences of an unbounded imagination happen all the time for those subjective adventurers who surf the synchronicities of life, the spiritualist cannot see the joy of the experience without their esoteric lollipop. The good news is once they get over the loss of their proverbial "Santa Claus," they are then able to settle into the natural world and recover from the *pressure* for the "need" of the fantasy.

Let's take another look at a quote from Shermer's book, *The Believing Brain:* [2]

> We form our beliefs for a variety of subjective, personal, emotional, and psychological reasons in the context of environments created by family, friends, colleagues, culture, and society at large; after forming our beliefs we then defend, justify, and rationalize them with a host of intellectual reasons, cogent arguments, and rational explanations. Beliefs come first; explanations follow.

In my early years, as an earnestly seeking novice, I had the uncomfortable pleasure of meeting a man named Lee. He was a mild-mannered man with a cryptic aura about him and a special talent for pushing the buttons of the faithful.

Because we worked in the same office digitizing embroidery designs for a living, we had plenty of time to talk about everything. Looking back, I realize the gift of this serendipitous relationship. Day after day, I talked to him about my spiritual beliefs, religion, metaphysics, UFO's and so on. Every now and then, Lee dropped a question that would shatter my assumed reality.

This continued for years and culminated in a close friendship. I learned from this experience that my beliefs were fragile. I had never been given the opportunity to sit with someone skilled in critical thinking. I was not taught how to inquire for myself, but how to believe. The interesting thing is that even though Lee was a critical thinker, he still expressed his emotions as freely as any spiritual person. The deconstructing process I went through was grueling to say the least. It took all I could muster to look at everything I considered true—to be a lie!

I remember asking Lee after the realization of my delusional certainties, "what do I do?" His reply will ring in my ears forever. He said, "Start over!" I said, "Do you mean throw everything I have learned out the window and begin again?" "Yep," he replied, "that simple!" This was the start of my radical investigation and belief deconstruction career. It did not happen overnight, but through a long and trying process I was able to come out of my orthodox and esoteric dilemma relatively unscathed.

I made this radical curiosity skill a part of my subjective toolbox as I proceeded on my metaphysical adventure. I began to look at the similarities from my Christian years and the pieces began to fit. I discovered that even though I was connected to a group of "open minded" spiritual folks that they were not immune to belief. Rather, I found they were deeply vested into belief, and in some cases, more than the obvious orthodox admissions. The cosmic story, interlaced with pseudo-scientific jargon, validated the misguided investigator. *Accept* and *trust* was the cosmic order, rather than *obey* and *worship* of the orthodox kind. Again, same face different mask.

What makes intelligence so threatening from a religious or spiritual perspective? Simply put—*inquiry shines the light on emotionally charged certainties*. Being truthful with ourselves is a challenging task, especially when we have been shamed or ridiculed for our deepest thoughts and emotions. We must fight for self-honesty and our native humanity and break down the delusions that *tempt our pretending*.

I think we should view spirituality like the poetry it is. Personally, I relish in the magical world of my Subjective. I wonder, in awe, at the vastness and depths of the universe. I breathe in the fire of life at sunrise and exhale with gratitude at its setting. I can create a host of angels or devils one moment and destroy them the next. I can invoke the great sages of all ages, draw insight from their presence, and send them away with a whisper. There is no limit to the magic at my fingertips, and yet I no longer assign these experiences to a literal invisible world, or dimension, filled with entities or gods. I can create a "God" if I choose, to invoke a sense of power or truth, but I know it is my creation. I know it does not exist outside my imagination. This idea is summed up beautifully in the words of Joseph Campbell:

> *Heaven and hell are within us, and all the Gods are within us. This is the great realization of the Upanishads of India in the ninth century B.C. All the Gods, all the heavens, all the worlds, are within us. They are magnified dreams, and dreams are manifestations in image form of <u>the energies of the body</u> in conflict with each other. That is what myth is. Myth is a manifestation in symbolic images, in metaphorical images, of the energies of the organs of the body in conflict with each other.*[4]

Chapter 19

LIVING IN REAL TIME

"Imagine how different dialogue might be with future generations raised on the idea that there are biological constraints on our ability to know what we know. To me, that is our only hope."
— Robert A. Burton

"He who thinks he knows doesn't know. He who knows he doesn't know, knows."
— Joseph Campbell

Living in real-time is not a concept. It is not the destination of some sacred or holy "now" moment. Living in real-time means living *as* the current of life is. It is living with who and what you are as a pulsing, moment to moment experience. It is all things included within your Subjective and objective awareness.

When you live life as a natural person you no longer hold yourself to some higher spiritual standard. You are free to be human, free to be yourself. Your natural instincts are no longer viewed as sinful or lower. You cognitively embrace your humanity, celebrate your biology and live with "ever present curiosity" because every moment is new. You are no longer living in the past or trapped in the imagined fears of a non-existent future. You understand the importance of living an authentic and ethical life *because* it is in the best interest of your species and your own survival. You are not measuring or comparing your life to a divine figure such as Jesus. You are yourself. You might do things differently than Mr. Messiah; perhaps you are not as nice as he was or perhaps you are nicer. You are not Gandhi, Buddha, or Quan Yin either. You are you, and your contribution to the world is one of a kind.

The programming of the spiritual systems injects a belief that we are less-than those great divine messengers—that we, are just not as close to their quality of character. Baloney! Each of us are a new evolutionary expression. It took millions of years to produce you, and your unique perspective is what these spiritual leaders don't have. Do you understand the brevity of this? You are the only one with your expression EVER in the history of the world. Perhaps Jesus wishes he, was you? Here's possibility thinking; maybe the eternal, stale, unchanging and boring god or goddess in the sky, wishes they were as authentic and unique as you. I say, abandon the requirements of the 'invisible you' with all of its self-depreciating ideas and relax into the 'physical you' as an evolved intelligent primate in its natural environment. Stand barefoot in the dirt, breathe in the fresh air, and sleep under the stars that reflect your endless unconscious.

Living in real-time is what is naturally happening without any concept or story. One is free to think and feel however they choose without attaching metaphysical conditions. It is just like being a kid again. When you are a kid, you are not segregating every thought and feeling. You are living and being the inquisitive primate that you are. A story or concept can be entertaining to play with as long as one does not forget who they are and *become* the story. This is an important distinction. Once you realize the difference, you can have fun with concepts, stories, and ideas because you are free to use them like colors on an artist's pallet.

Polish-American scientist and philosopher Alfred Korzybski who wrote, "General Semantics," is best known for his dictum, "The map is not the territory."

> The map–territory connection is the relationship between an object and a representation of that object, as in the relation between a geographical territory and a map of it—that an abstraction drawn from something, or a reaction to it, is not the thing itself. Korzybski held that people tend to confuse maps with territories they describe. It is describing identification with the mental image versus the actual thing itself which must be experienced in the real world. There is reality, and there are our models of reality.[1]

Humans who are stuck in the concepts of themselves and the world, miss the "ground of being" (biology) to which those concepts point. The spiritual map was intended to help us cope with the natural world, to relieve the anxiety of death, and *suspend* for a time, but not *replace*—reality.

One of the key stepping stones on my journey toward greater awareness was the subject of non-duality and free will. The message of non-dualism does not require belief, nor is it necessary to subscribe to any theories for it to be effective. It is a method of observation and realization that leads to the deconstruction or dissolution of the illusory self. Sound simple? Not quite.

There is a little bombshell in the non-duality teaching that unlocks its treasure—it is non-volition. From a non-dualist point of view, "you" are a figment of your imagination. There is no volitional entity in the human skull that makes decisions and no personal author that orchestrates the impulses of life. Because we evolved over time, the idea of a volitional-self is just plain silly, unless you create a *story* of an invisible you which is even sillier. Non-duality fits nicely into the model of the human primate. The character in the mind, that humans think is in control of their lives, is the same character who believes itself to be eternal and exist in other realms.

By understanding and experimenting with this idea, one can easily find that free will appears more like an illusion than a reality. Consider for a moment how much free will you actually have. Who wakes up in the morning? Is it you? Did "you" make the wake-up plans during sleep? Who gets tired and hungry? Who chooses to go to the bathroom? Who decides to feel aroused? Is it the little man or woman inside your head making all these decisions? Are you breathing or are you *being breathed?*

A study conducted by scientists from the Max Planck Institute for Human Cognitive and Brain Sciences in Leipzig, Germany explores this concept:

> Already several seconds before we consciously make a decision its outcome can be predicted from unconscious activity in the brain. In the study, participants could freely decide if they wanted to press a button with their left or right hand. They were free to make this decision whenever they wanted but had to remember at which time they felt they had made up their mind. The aim of the experiment was to find out what happens in the brain in the period just before the person felt the decision was made. The researchers found that it was possible to predict, from brain signals, which option participants would take already seven seconds before they

> consciously made their decision. Normally researchers look at what happens when the decision is made, but not at what happens several seconds before. The fact that decisions can be predicted so long before they are made is an astonishing finding.[2]

I think the above description raises the bar for who and what we are in the grand scheme of things. With biology making the calls, the volitional spirit self now has an even bigger fish to fry; one that eliminates its entire story. Bestselling author and neuroscientist, Sam Harris, articulately expands on this idea in his book Free Will:

> I generally start each day with a cup of coffee or tea—sometimes two. This morning, it was coffee (two). Why not tea? I am in no position to know. I wanted coffee more than I wanted tea today, and I was free to have what I wanted. Did I consciously choose coffee over tea? No. The choice was made for me by events in my brain that I, as the conscious witness of my thoughts and actions, could not inspect or influence. Could I have "changed my mind" and switched to tea before the coffee drinker in me could get his bearings? Yes, but this impulse would also have been the product of unconscious causes. Why didn't it arise this morning? Why might it arise in the future? I cannot know. The intention to do one thing and not another does not originate in consciousness, rather, it appears in consciousness, as does any thought or impulse that might oppose it.[3]

This realization puts an axe to the foot of the spiritual tree. It is effective for breaking the trance of identification with the spiritual phantom because it is a statement of truth—not the kind of truth that requires belief—but experiential truth. If it can lead a person to the realization of their inherent existence, then I think they have arrived at the destination. No longer are the enlightened guru's powers effective. There is no need to buy the story or get duped by the tricksters. Seekers are looking for a way to make sense of things, and because the spiritual quest is born out of erroneous teachings, childhood trauma, and a shamed imagination, critical thinking and the knowledge of evolution lift the weary traveler to greater heights.

One of the most unSpiritual teachers of our time is author Jed McKenna. His book, *"Spiritual Enlightenment: The Damnedest Thing,"* kicked off a Zen whooping for the Spiritual community. It was this book (the first of three) that drove the stake through the heart of metaphysics for me and prepared the ground for a non-dualistic natural existence. For people who have been on the spiritual path for a while and feel stuck in their tracks or are sensing the need to break out of old non-human habit patterns, I recommend his work.

Here is an excerpt:

> Enlightenment is selfless awareness. The process of enlightenment is not about becoming who you really are but about unbecoming who you never were. It cannot be desired or wished for because prior to its achievement, failure is pre-ordained by the radical deconstruction of self-required to slip from the grip of the intolerable lie of self. From the perspective of ego, enlightenment is the biggest nothing of all

> time, totally anti-climactic, like waking up
> from a spectacular dream.[4]

It is not the aim of this writing to explore the depths of the above topic, but it is on the radar for a follow up book. I hope to explain, in detail, how it is that I can have the exact same spiritual experiences without the former esoteric glue attached. I believe we *are* the magic as natural human primates and when we truly understand our connection to the natural world, our abilities will appear like flowers in a long-awaited garden . . . *whose seeds have laid dormant for eons.*

We are a part of something unimaginably vaster than our illusory spiritual identity. The impulses of the human primate, the intelligence, intuition and almost 6th sense acuteness to the environment and people are all owed to the slow and sure process of evolution. There is no credit to give an invisible self. There is no "one" who authors this activity. You as a volitional concept are an illusion. You, as a human primate are real. It pretty much boils down to that. Your drives and inclinations are part of an evolutionary continuum that you, as a self-aware primate, can experience. It's fantastic when you remove the "I" and realize you never had anything to do with it in the first place. This puts birth and death out of your hands as well.

> *Never were you born, and never will you die,*
> *For there never was a "you" in the first place.*

Chapter 20

THE FOCUSING METHOD

"Your physically-felt body is in fact part of a Gigantic system of here and other places, now and other times, you and other people—in fact, the whole universe. This sense of being bodily alive in a vast system is the body as it is felt from inside."
— Eugene T. Gendlin

This chapter, most assuredly, is my favorite chapter because it offers an effective and simple method for freeing oneself from subjective trappings which opens the door for developing an amazing relationship with yourself.

The Focusing method was developed by Eugene Gendlin[1] who conducted a 15-year study analyzing the effectiveness of psychotherapy. He discovered that the success of therapy had more to do with how the patient behaved than the therapist's technique. He found that what the patient *does* inside him or herself was the constant for progress. He noticed how talk therapy kept patients "thinking" about their problems rather than accessing the root issue.

In every case, the patient who focused deeply inside themselves, on a subtle intuitive level, (a "felt" bodily sense) were able to uncover information that held the keys to their resolution.

Focusing is a simple skill to learn. It is a natural process that can easily become second nature after a little practice. It teaches you how to consciously live from the inside out rather than the outside in—living from your core truth. Once learned, it is yours for a lifetime and can be passed on to others in a simple conversation.

The "felt sense" is a name Eugene coined which represents the pre-verbal sense of "something" in the subjective environment. The deep awareness inside that has not been brought to the surface of conscious thought. It is a bodily awareness of a situation such as an old hurt or fear of or perhaps an idea or insight. It is always *more* than verbal expression. Most importantly, it is that which is *vague and unclear*.

Focusing is as natural as breathing. We humans do it on a regular basis, but we tend to remedy inner discomfort by talking, drinking, smoking, entertainment, sex and other distractions. What focusing teaches us is that our inner experience is a language, it is information offering insight and guidance. The painful emotions and negative thoughts are messages, signals, trying to bring to our attention something that which is in our best interest to understand.

The following is from the Focusing Institute's website on the six essential steps for learning how to focus.

> The inner act of focusing can be broken down into six main sub-acts or movements. As you gain more practice, you won't need to think of these as six separate parts of the process. To think of them as separate movements makes the process seem more mechanical than it is, or will be, for you later.
>
> I have subdivided the process in this way because I've learned from years of experimenting that this is one of the effective ways to teach focusing to people who have never tried it before.

Think of this as only the basics. As you progress and learn more about focusing you will add to these basic instructions, clarify them, approach them from other angles. Eventually, perhaps not the first time you go through it, you will have the experience of something shifting inside.

So here are the focusing instructions in brief form, manual style. If you want to try them out, do so easily, gently. If you find difficulty in one step or another, don't push too hard, just move on to the next one. You can always come back.

Clearing a space
What I will ask you to do will be silent, just to yourself. Take a moment just to relax. All right—now, inside you, I would like you to pay attention inwardly, in your body, perhaps in your stomach or chest. Now see what comes *there* when you ask, "How is my life going?" "What is the main thing for me right now?" Sense within your body. Let the answers come slowly from this sensing. When some concern comes, do not go inside it! Stand back and say, "Yes, that's there. I can feel that, there." Let there be a little space between *you and that*. Then ask what else you feel. Wait again, and sense. Usually there are several things.

Felt Sense
From among what came, select one personal problem to focus on. Do not go inside it! Stand back from it. Of course, there are many parts to that one thing you are thinking about—too many

to think of each one alone. But you can *feel* all of these things together. Pay attention there where you usually feel things, and in there you can get a sense of what *all of the problem* feels like. Let yourself feel the unclear sense of *all of that.*

Handle
What is the quality of this unclear felt sense? Let a word, a phrase, or an image come up from the felt sense itself. It might be a quality-word, like *tight, sticky, scary, stuck, heavy, jumpy* or a phrase, or an image. Stay with the quality of the felt sense till something fits it just right.

Resonating
Go back and forth between the felt sense and the word (phrase, or image). Check how they resonate with each other. See if there is a little bodily signal that lets you know there is a fit. To do it, you have to have the felt sense there again, as well as the word. Let the felt sense change, if it does, and also the word or picture, until they feel just right in capturing the quality of the felt sense.

Asking
Now ask, what is it about this whole problem that makes this quality (which you have just named or pictured)? Make sure the quality is sensed again, freshly, vividly (not just remembered from before). When it is here again, tap it, touch it, be with it, asking, "What makes the whole problem so _____?" Or ask, "What is in *this* sense?" If you get a quick answer without a shift in the felt sense, just let that kind of answer go by. Return your attention to your

body and freshly find the felt sense again. Then ask it again. Be with the felt sense till something comes along with a shift, a slight "give" or release.

Receiving
Receive whatever comes with a shift in a friendly way. Stay with it a while, even if it is only a slight release. Whatever comes, this is only one shift; there will be others. You will probably continue after a little while but stay here for a few moments. If during these instructions, somewhere you have spent a little while sensing and touching an unclear holistic body sense of this problem, then you have focused. It doesn't matter whether the body-shift came or not. It comes on its own. We don't control that.[2]

There are numerous books on Focusing and you can find informative videos and articles on their website. I hope this short introduction sparks your interest in developing a relationship with your whole self. I truly believe that the world is lived from the inside out and that "war" begins within human beings who project what they reject inside. This method called "Focusing" is one of the most important tools for our species. I also recommend Byron Katie's "The Work" which you can learn more about at the website (www.thework.com).

We are a species that has become trapped in our inner world. This has resulted in the creation of a painful world. Use these methods for breaking identification patterns and pass them on to others along your way. They are tools for a lifetime—pearls without price.

CONCLUSION

"Man is born to live, not to prepare for life."
— Boris Pasternak

"Somewhere, something incredible is waiting to be known."
— Carl Sagan

"We must be willing to let go of the life we planned so as to have the life that is waiting for us."
— Joseph Campbell

I left my childhood like a damaged satellite, smoking, spinning out of control, and crash landing onto a planet called spirituality. I traveled across the terrain looking for the answers to the big questions—who am I, where did I come from, why am I here and where am I going? The discoveries on this trip would later explain the fire burning in my genes. "I Am Primate" was an unexpected awakening—an opening into a vast new world lying just beneath my skin. It is a remarkable thing to awaken from a trance on your own home planet. In a future book, I plan on writing my unSpiritual story. I hope it will encourage others to write theirs and share the wisdom of the lost primates.

So where do we go from here? The best answer I can suggest is to do your own digging. Use this fantastic tool we call the worldwide web to probe into cutting-edge research. Make a hobby of it. Explore the wealth of knowledge at your fingertips. Ask bolder questions. Study subjects like trans-humanism, interstellar space travel, and nanotechnology—just a few subjects that are ripe for the inquisitive explorer. Get involved in humanitarian efforts and help solve the many problems that plague our world. In other words, do something—engage the adventure! Your questions will rest in the satisfaction of your efforts until answered.

Be yourself, trust yourself, and acknowledge all of yourself as one person. Develop your radical curiosity and learn how to navigate the Subjective with the awe and humility of a skilled warrior. Sharpen your sword daily. Trust in the ability to question things and don't be afraid to call a thing as you see it. Free yourself from the delusion of certainty and ground your speculations in peer reviewed science and critical-thinking. It is the earned gift of our species.

Don't get caught in the trap of thought prejudice. Realize that life is "thinking and feeling" which is *one whole intelligence*. The brain doesn't say to the heart "you're too mushy today" and the heart does not reply "get out of your head." We are segregated by our beliefs which are built on erroneous outdated information. Don't split your internal world into parts. Accept yourself as a biological ecosystem wrapped up in one spectacular evolutionary achievement. Celebrate this moment and nurture both the dark and light sides of your being as one spiral of information—one organic, intelligent whole, rather than segregated parts.

Don't let the dualist philosophy split you in two with their pious, pompous, spiritual babble. When they are being presumptuous, consider that they might be in a trance trying to dominate your thinking to validate their feeling.

Honor your species. Study ethics and value altruism. Learn from the brilliant minds of our time and study their humanitarian efforts. We no longer live in tribes, but on a planet full of people with common needs. Develop new ideas for a better world, not for some imaginary place after death.

Write a book, poem, or song. There is plenty to do, a myriad of problems to fix, and a host of riddles to solve. You are one of a kind, and the only one with your perspective. You may not be an evolutionary biologist or neurologist, but your human skills by default qualify you to solve problems in our world.

Develop your skeptical side. Use your imagination to solve problems in our world. Design new plans for world peace, craft wonderful music, poetry and art. Turn your internal battle into an outflow of creativity to the world and your community, your family and friends. "Be" the creative human being life made you to be over so many millions of years. You owe it to those who have come before you. We owe it to all life, whether it has a purpose or not. Life grows, solves problems and flourishes. So do you!

> *"We stand on the shoulders of the many who came before us, who fought for reason, and broke the chains of religious ideology and authoritarian decree. Ode to the thinking men and women of our past who have led us down the road to reason in a world of superstition. They have been the harbingers of reason and the hope for our species."*

Thank You
Christopher Loren

Healing Our World

*It is my hope that humanity will awaken to
who they are as a species.*

*That they will no longer relinquish the problems of the
world to the domain of the Gods.*

That they will begin to care for each other.

*That they will begin to heal the world today,
And not wait until tomorrow.*

*That they will never give themselves another excuse to
justify non-action for the survival of their kind.*

*That they will stop deferring their innate intelligence to
invisible properties.*

*That they will stand up and be human and be proud of
their evolutionary origins.*

*That they will honor their world and each other through
the realization of their shared genetic tree.*

*That they would understand their connection to the
natural world like a fish to water.*

*That my species, will see the world's problems as
"their" problems, and be the change for the
survival of their own kind.*

*And finally, may they give themselves and everyone else,
permission to be human.*

Christopher Loren

NOTES

Chapter 1

[1] http://en.wikipedia.org/wiki/The_Wizard_of_Oz_(1939_film) (Retrieved March 9, 2013)

Chapter 2

[1] William Arntz, Betsy Chasse, Mark Vicente., *"What the Bleep Do We Know"* Publisher - Health Communications Inc. ©2005 Captured Light Distributions, LLC

[2] *"Spirituality,"* Merriam-Webster.com. 2013. http://www.merriam-webster.com (Retrieved March 9, 2013)

[3] Ewert Cousins, preface to Antoine Faivre and Jacob Needleman, *"Modern Esoteric Spirituality,"* Crossroad Publishing 1992.

[4] Philip Sheldrake, *"A Brief History of Spirituality,"* Wiley-Blackwell; 1 edition.

[5] Margaret A. Burkhardt and Mary Gail Nagai-Jacobson, *"Spirituality: living our connectedness,"* Delmar Cengage Learning; 1 edition.

[6] Kees Waaijman, *"Spirituality: forms, foundations, methods"* Leuven: Peeters, 2002 p. 1

[7] "Spirit" Online Etymology Dictionary, 2001-2012. http://www.etymonline.com (Retrieved March 9, 2013)

[8] Victor J. Stenger, *"The New Atheism: Taking a Stand for Science and Reason"* Prometheus Books.

[9] Todd Murphy, 2013, *"The Beginnings of Spirituality and Death Anxiety in Human Evolution"* http://www.shaktitechnology.com/deathanxiety.htm (Retrieved March 9, 2013)

[10] "Subjective". dictionary.com. 2013.
http://dictionary.reference.com (Retrieved March 9, 2013)

Chapter 3

[1] Allan Kardec *(2010) The Spirit's Book*, Spiritualist Classics.

[2] YouTube, *"Does God Have a Future? Nightline debate"*
http://www.youtube.com/watch?v=wi2IC6e5DUY (Retrieved March 9, 2013)

[3] Stenger, Victor J. *"The New Atheism: Taking a Stand for Science and Reason"* Prometheus Books.

[4] Harris, Sam *"Response to Controversy,"*
http://www.samharris.org/site/full_text/response-to-controversy2/ (Retrieved March 9, 2013)

[5] Gorenfeld, John (2004-09-16). *"Bleep" of faith"*.
http://www.salon.com/2004/09/16/bleep_2/. (Retrieved March 9, 2013)

[6] Stenger, Victor J., (1993), *"The Myth of Quantum Consciousness"* The Humanist, Vol. 53, No. 3

[7] Ramesh S. Balsekar, *"The Wisdom of Balsekar: The Essence of Enlightenment from the World's Leading Teacher of Advaita"* Watkins.

[8] M. A. Persinger (1993) Vectorial Cerebral Hemisphericity As Differential Sources For The Sensed Presence, Mystical Experiences And Religious Conversions. Perceptual And Motor Skills: Volume 76, Issue , Pp. 915-930.

[9] V.S. Ramachandran, M.D., PH.D., and Sandra Blakeslee - *"Phantoms in the Brain"* New York: William Morror, 1998.

Chapter 4

[1] Elan Golomb PH.D. *"Trapped in the Mirror: Adult Children of Narcissists in their Struggle for Self"* William Morrow & Company, Inc.

[2] Robert Monroe *"Journeys Out of the Body"* Broadway Books; Updated edition.

[3] Thomas Metzinger, *"The Ego Tunnel: The Science of the Mind and the Myth of the Self"* Basic Books; First Trade Paper Edition edition.

[4] Michael Shermer, *"The Believing Brain: From Ghosts and Gods to Politics and Conspiracies---How We Construct Beliefs and Reinforce Them as Truths"* Times Books.

Chapter 5

[1] http://en.wikipedia.org/wiki/J._Z._Knight#Ramtha (Retrieved March 9, 2013)

[2] Sagan, Carl (March 1997). *"The Demon-Haunted World: Science as a Candle in the Dark"* Ballantine Books. pp. 480.

Chapter 7

[1] http://focusing.org/ (Retrieved July 7, 2013)

[2] Christopher S. Hyatt, *"Undoing Yourself with Energized Meditation & Other Devices,"* The Original Falcon Press; 10th edition.

Chapter 8

[1] http://en.wikipedia.org/wiki/Dweller_on_the_threshold (Retrieved March 9, 2013)

Chapter 9

[1] Rick Potts and Chris Sloan, *"What Does It Mean to Be Human?"* National Geographic

[2] http://en.wikipedia.org/wiki/Human (Retrieved March 9, 2013)

Chapter 13

[1] Watson, Burton (1999), *"The Zen Teachings of Master Lin-Chi: A Translation of the Lin-chi lu,"* New York: Columbia University Press.

[2] Victor J. Stenger, *"God and the Folly of Faith: The Incompatibility of Science and Religion"* Prometheus Books Inc.

Chapter 14

[1] From: Nora Bunce, Eastern Cherokee, Date: 21 February 1995 - New Agers and native wisdom - A dialog on the NATCHAT list, February 1995 - http://www.hartford-hwp.com/archives/41/021.html (Retrieved March 9, 2013)

Chapter 16

[1] http://en.wikipedia.org/wiki/Observer_effect_(physics) (Retrieved March 9, 2013)

[2] Steven Pinker *"The Better Angels of Our Nature: Why Violence Has Declined"* Penguin Books; Reprint edition.

Chapter 17

[1] http://www.venganza.org/ (Retrieved March 9, 2013)

[2] Humberto Maturana Romesin and Gerda Verden-Zoller, *"Biology Of Love"* Opp, G.: Peterander, F. (Hrsg.): Focus Heilpadagogik, Ernst Reinhardt, Munchen/Basel 1996.

Chapter 18

[1] Robert Burton *"On Being Certain: Believing You Are Right Even When You're Not"* St. Martin's Press; First Edition edition.

[2] Michael Shermer *"The Believing Brain: From Ghosts and Gods to Politics and Conspiracies---How We Construct Beliefs and Reinforce Them as Truths"* St. Martin's Griffin.

[3] http://www.focusing.org (Retrieved August 3, 2013)

[4] Joseph. Campbell *"THE POWER OF MYTH with Bill Moyers"* Doubleday; 1st edition (1988)

Chapter 19

[1] http://en.wikipedia.org/wiki/General_semantics (Retrieved March 9, 2013)

[2] http://www.mpg.de/en (Retrieved March 9, 2013)

[3] Sam Harris, *"Free Will"* Free Press; Original edition.

[4] Jed McKenna, *"Spiritual Enlightenment: The Damnedest Thing"* Wisefool Press.

Chapter 20

[1] http://www.focusing.org (Retrieved August 3, 2013)

[2] http://www.focusing.org/sixsteps.html (Retrieved August 3, 2013)

Printed in Great Britain
by Amazon